Getting into

Oxford &
Cambridge

2011 Entry

'Getting into' guides

Getting into

Oxford &
Cambridge

2011 Entry

Katy Blatt

13th edition

Getting into Oxford & Cambridge: 2011 Entry

This 13th edition published in 2010 by Trotman Publishing, an imprint of Crimson Publishing Limited, Westminster House, Kew Road, Richmond, Surrey TW9 2ND

© Trotman Publishing 2008, 2009, 2010
© Trotman & Co Ltd 1987, 1989, 1991, 1994, 1996, 1999, 2001, 2003, 2005, 2007

Author: Katy Blatt

12th edition by Sarah Alakija
11th edition by Natalie Lancer
Editions 7–10 by Sarah Alakija

British Library Cataloguing in Publication Data
A catalogue record for this book is available from the British Library.

ISBN: 978–1–84455–238–2

Typeset by IDSUK (DataConnection) Ltd
Printed and bound in the UK by TJ International Ltd, Padstow, Cornwall

Contents

About the author

After learning the violin with a teacher at the Royal College of Music in London, Katy Blatt studied art history at Cambridge University between 2003 and 2006. She graduated from the Courtauld Institute of Art in London in 2008 with an MA degree in 'Art and Cultural Politics in Germany, 1890–1945' after having co-curated the 'East Wing VIII – On Time' Exhibition (January 2008–July 2009) at Somerset House. She subsequently interned at the Museum of Modern Art in New York, where she helped research the recent Miró exhibition, and worked as the 'Schools and Teachers' intern at Tate Britain in their Youth Programmes Department. She has also worked as an educator at the Soane Museum in London (2007–2009). In March 2009 she began working at the MPW School, London, where she teaches art history and English language to 16–19 year olds.

Acknowledgements

Many thanks should go to all those who have previously written the Trotman guide to *Getting into Oxford and Cambridge*, particularly Sarah Alakija, on whose 2009 edition I have loosely based the information in this book on. Thanks also to John Meeske, Jim Burnett, Matthew Judd, Valeria Givone, Elaine Miles and Natasha Grabov, Amy Thomas, Freyja Cox Jensen, George Marshall and Sarah Kemsley for their advice.

Foreword

When I applied to Cambridge for the first time in 2001 I was 17 years old and pretty clueless. I wasn't really sure what I wanted to study at university. However, I did know, absolutely, that I wanted to go to Cambridge. I knew that what I loved more than anything in the world was to learn, to read, and to explore ideas; and I wanted to be some-where that would foster these feelings. I knew about the special intel-lectual environment at Cambridge because I had been born there (whilst my father was completing his post-doctoral research) and I wanted a piece of it for myself.

I applied to read history at Clare College, and, perhaps unsurprisingly, didn't get in. I was in the middle of my A levels and family upheavals, and I hadn't thought through my application. I loved history at school, but I hadn't done much extra reading. I hadn't formulated my own opinions and there-fore I hadn't been able to express myself with confidence at interview.

I was devastated when I received the letter of rejection: 'We are sorry to inform you that, upon careful consideration . . .' I sat on my bed in shock for about an hour and then pulled myself together. I looked at other universities, but there was nowhere else I wanted to go. I decided to take a gap year and to reapply having prepared more thoroughly.

When I went back to school the following day, my art teacher suggested that I apply for a subject called art history – something that was not offered at my school. I read Gombrich's *The Story of Art* and had an immediate sense that this discipline would suit me perfectly. I loved art, I loved history and I loved people. This was a subject that combined politics, sociology, history, psychoanalysis and visual appreciation. What more could I ask for?

During my gap year I studied the violin at the Royal College of Music and practised for seven hours a day, every day. In the time I wasn't practising, I read and read about art history. My boyfriend's father was an architect, and I devoured every architectural history book on his shelves. I spent hours in the library, I went to every gallery and exhibition in every city I passed through, and I told everyone I met about what I was reading. I was determined that, by the time I went back to interview, I would know what I was talking about.

Towards the end of my gap year my grandmother suggested that I get some interview practice and directed me to the company Oxbridge Applications, who offer mock interviews. I signed up, and with trepidation attended several days of excellent interview practice. These mock interviews helped me overcome the anxiety I felt when talking to strangers about my subject, and prepared me for the type of questions I might be asked. When I was called to interview at Girton College, Cambridge in 2002 I set off with my four As at A level secured, a mature understanding of my chosen subject and a confident attitude.

When I arrived for interview I was relieved to find that, for every question I was asked, I had a considered answer to give. There were no strange questions or uncomfortable moments, just an interesting discussion which confirmed in my mind how much I wanted to learn more about this subject. The interviewers seemed to see this. I was in!

At Cambridge I met lots of intelligent and exciting young people: some of my best friends to this day. Most people who study there are ambitious and want to 'make a difference' in some way, and it was intensely satisfying as well as exhilarating to live in that environment. It was also incredibly exciting to have the freedom to explore. With only five hours of lectures a week and two hours of supervisions, I could organise my time as I wished. Most of my time was spent researching and writing essays, but I managed to squeeze in time to lead the violin section in the university orchestra, sing in the college choir, attend my friends' philosophy lectures, and generally investigate other subjects.

Everyone applies to Oxbridge expecting to work harder than they ever have before. Sometimes I felt that my personal life was crushed under the sheer weight of expectation from supervisors and competition with peers. The level of stress was continuously high throughout the eight-week terms, and during holidays there was always more reading and writing to do in preparation for the next term. Some people didn't cope well. The combination of living in a new environment away from home and the intensity of the work schedule meant that they became ill, depressed, or simply gave up. Half way through the first term I was seriously considering going back to music college. However once I got into the swing of things, the intellectual excitement of the place got to me like a drug that I didn't want to give up.

My three years at Cambridge were simultaneously gruelling, exhausting and wonderful. I read more, and faster, than I ever had before, until sometimes I could practically feel my skull expanding. The quality of the academic support I was given (from my wonderful director of studies at King's, Jean Michel Massing) is, to this day, the best I have had in my life, and with this I found my intellectual confidence growing. The speed with which we were expected to produce essays was awesome (I had written four 2,500 word essays before my friends at other universities had written their first!), so in order to cope, we all had to develop an ability to process and analyse information quickly. I emerged in the summer of 2006 as if out of some intellectual boot camp, feeling that I had had one of the most academically rigorous trainings in the world.

My arts degree at Cambridge did not prepare me for the 'world of work'. I have had to struggle with the transition from university to working life as much as any other recent graduate. The skills needed in graduate-level jobs are often not academic but practical, and an undergraduate degree in the arts from Cambridge is anything but practical. However, everyone knows – universities and employers – that the standard of Oxbridge graduates is very high. Oxbridge graduates are thought to be fast learners and speedy thinkers; people who are good at organising and communicating ideas. If we don't know how to do something at first, employers can be sure that we will find out very swiftly. For this reason, there is no doubt that a training at Oxford and Cambridge gains graduates positive recognition from employers and creates many opportunities that would not otherwise open up.

This book is intended to give bright young people some facts about the Oxbridge system, and to demystify the application processes. There should not be secrets here, just hard work, dedication, and excitement about learning. I hope this book helps to create many more opportunities for talented students, and I wish every reader luck in their quest for knowledge.

Katy Blatt, December 2009

Introduction
Why apply to Oxbridge?

Oxford and Cambridge are the oldest universities in the United Kingdom. Founded in 1096 and in 1209 respectively by monastic orders, both universities have a wealth of history that pervades every courtyard. In both Oxford and Cambridge, the universities form the hub of what were once medieval towns, and the students who live and work there are central to the vibrant life of both cities. Famous for their obscure traditions, you may have heard stories about undergraduates in dinner jackets at candlelit tables, extravagant drinking rituals, masked balls in the summer when the banks of the River Cam are lit by fireworks, and the secret societies whose members meet at midnight. This air of mystery is often propagated by the academics who work at Oxford and Cambridge, perhaps because they enjoy the sense of authenticity and grandeur that this brings them. It is certainly true that, for hundreds of years, Oxford and Cambridge have attracted the most prestigious scholars in the world: Einstein and Steven Hawking to name only two. However, does this past grandeur and historical prestige translate into a world-class modern university education? Following are some of the reasons why Oxford and Cambridge are still two of the best educational institutions in the world, and why they are worth applying to.

Perhaps one of the most distinctive features of an Oxbridge education, and one that is unique to these two institutions, is the **tutorial/supervision system**. Tutorials (at Oxford) and supervisions (at Cambridge) are hour-long, weekly meetings that take place between one or two students and a member of the academic teaching staff at the students' college. These meetings are attended in addition to a related lecture series and are meant to add to students' knowledge of the subjects they are already studying. Essays and additional reading/problems to solve are set by the supervisor or tutor during the meetings as homework. The following week, the marked work and/or reading form the main topics of discussion.

This hour of academic mentoring offers intellectual nourishment that is generally unavailable at other universities. It is a rare privilege to get this degree of personal attention and intellectual support, and students usually feel well cared for as well as learning a great deal from their teachers and colleagues. At these meetings students have the opportunity to discuss the strengths and weaknesses of their essays in detail, to ask questions about ideas they find interesting or confusing, and to learn to defend their arguments convincingly in person. This system also encourages students to develop their communication skills, to gain confidence when debating their point, and to listen to constructive criticism.

The **collegiate system** is also almost completely unique to Oxbridge. Oxford and Cambridge are two very large universities (Oxford has about 11,500 undergraduate students and Cambridge about 10,500), but these vast institutions are made more cosy and personal through their division into colleges. Instead of applying to the university as a whole, prospective Oxbridge students normally apply to an individual college. Consisting of a food hall, where meals are prepared three times a day; bedrooms, which are cleaned daily; laundry rooms; and a bar, where students meet to unwind in the evenings; a student's college environment often forms the centre of his/her social life. Porters, stationed at the door of each college, watch the comings and goings of students, prevent the general public from intruding, and generally keep a watchful eye on the behaviour of 'freshers' (new students). Leaving home for the first time can be stressful and overwhelming, and the social and pastoral network provided by the college creates a safe and comfortable environment in which to experience this transition.

The college also forms the hub of a student's academic life. Each undergraduate at Cambridge is assigned a director of studies (DOS) and at Oxford, a tutor: a senior academic who is responsible for the intellectual development of their students. DOSs and tutors usually have their offices in the grounds of the college, and can easily be called upon for help and advice. Although students sit exams with the rest of the university and may use university-wide resources (such as the university library) they benefit from the close contact of a small institution. Each college also has its own finances office, permanent staff and policies, and a surprising amount of autonomy and character.

There is no doubt that both Oxford and Cambridge offer a world-class education to this day. The **calibre of academics** and teaching staff at Oxford and Cambridge is equal to the best in the world, and comparable to institutions such as Harvard and Yale in the United States. In 2009 *The Times Good University Guide* placed Oxford and Cambridge first and second respectively in the UK for teaching quality and student achievement. The 2009 *Guardian University Guide* rankings also place Oxford and Cambridge in first and second place in the UK, and in the 2008 THES-QS World University Rankings, Cambridge was ranked second amongst world universities (behind Harvard) and Oxford was ranked fourth.

The list of distinguished people who have been educated at Oxbridge is huge: 40 prime ministers, including Margaret Thatcher and Tony Blair; at least 30 other international leaders including the current Archbishop of Canterbury and the Prime Minister of India; countless authors, including Oscar Wilde, Philip Pullman and J R R Tolkein; the famous scientists,

Stephen Hawking, Richard Dawkins (of *The God Delusion*) and Tim Berners-Lee (the co-inventor of the World Wide Web); the actors Hugh Grant, Michael Palin; and the filmmaker Ken Loach all kick-started their careers, spending three years of their lives beneath the beautiful cloisters of Oxford and Cambridge. Not only is Oxbridge a hub of academic excellence and superb tutoring, but it is also a nucleus of ideas, creative thinking and networking.

01 Equal opportunities
Am I eligible to apply?

Cambridge and Oxford are two of the leading universities in the world, but this does not mean they are unattainable. Their sole criterion for accepting new undergraduates is academic excellence. This is assessed through academic qualifications, but also during interviews and through special written tests prior to interview. If you have good academic qualifications and want to learn you are eligible and welcome to apply.

Fees, financial support and bursaries

Tuition fees

As with other universities in England, Cambridge and Oxford charge an annual tuition fee for students coming from within the UK. This amounts to £3,225 per year for the 2009–10 entry. A student loan can be taken out to cover this cost and the amount does not have to be repaid until you are earning more than £15,000 per year.

Living expenses

Living costs are heavily subsidised at Oxford and Cambridge. Room rental at both universities is normally between £70 and £85 per week, and students do not have to pay during holidays if they go home. Room rental also includes the cost of electricity and hot water. You may choose to buy your own food and cook for yourself, and there is usually a small charge per term for the use of a college kitchen. Alternatively there are three meals each day provided by every college's food 'halls', and these are subsidised: generally a three-course meal will cost no more than £3.

Financial support

Financial support is available for students who might find it difficult to afford to go to university. Both universities make it very clear that they are primarily interested in students' academic abilities, and not their socio-economic background.

As the Oxford prospectus explains:

If you can get in, we can help out . . . At Oxford your mind is the only asset we're interested in.

Oxford Prospectus, 2009

The Cambridge University website describes the Cambridge Bursary Scheme:

'We are committed to the principle that no UK student should be deterred from applying to the University of Cambridge because of financial concerns, and that no student should have to leave because of financial difficulties. As a result we have one of the most extensive financial support programmes in the UK to ensure that students can meet the cost of the Cambridge education, regardless of background'.

Cambridge Prospectus, Guide for Parents and Supporters, 2009. (www.cam.ac.uk/admissions/ undergraduate/publications/parentsguide.pdf)

Bursaries at both universities are worth approximately £12,000–£14,000 and these are made available to students in financial distress. In addition, most of the colleges have large endowments and can provide their own bursaries, grants and scholarships to students who are in need or who are exceptionally academically gifted. Financial rewards are given to students who achieve highly in exams, and most colleges will provide funding for travel in the summer holidays if the excursion is relevant to your studies.

Although both universities have an umbrella policy for supporting students financially, each college has different resources at its disposal. Therefore, you need to ring the admissions tutor at each college separately to ask their advice on the issue. For more information follow the links below.

Cambridge:

- bursaries and financial support: www.newtontrust.cam.ac.uk/ world/cbs/2009/funding
- financial information: www.cam.ac.uk/admissions/undergraduate/ finance/support

Oxford:

- bursaries and financial support: www.ox.ac.uk/admissions/ undergraduate_courses/student_funding
- financial information: www.cam.ac.uk/admissions/undergraduate/ finance/support

Music awards and scholarships

These are awarded to exceptionally talented musicians. Both Oxford and Cambridge are renowned for the high quality of music that they foster. Each college has a chapel which holds daily or weekly services and most colleges have two organ scholars and a choir. Singers must be of semi-professional standard and dedicate up to six hours a week to rehearsals. Both organ scholarships and choral scholarships are very competitive, but are worth up to several thousand pounds a year depending on which college you apply to. At Cambridge, each college gives annual instrumental awards amounting to several hundred pounds per year, as well as a chamber music scheme where students are trained by the university's resident quartet and are awarded an annual stipend. The size of the stipend depends upon the college's wealth and funding priorities. At Oxford, in addition to choral scholarships, there are also repetiteur scholarships. The application deadline for these awards is in September of the year before you are due to start at university (a month before the UCAS deadline for Oxbridge).

Cambridge:

- for choral and organ scholarships go to: www.cam.ac.uk/admissions/undergraduate/musicawards/organ
- for instrumental awards: www.cam.ac.uk/admissions/undergraduate/musicawards/instrumental

Oxford:

- download a leaflet for organ, choral and repetiteur (musical theatre) scholarships at: www.music.ox.ac.uk/admissions/organ-and-choral-scholarships

Mature and young students

Neither Cambridge nor Oxford specify a minimum or maximum age at which students can apply, so all committed and academically capable students are welcome. However, some colleges may be wary of accepting you if you are 16 years old or younger at the time of application, simply because they are concerned you may not be mature enough to cope with the university environment. You should telephone the admissions tutors at your college if you are 16 or under, to discuss this matter.

A mature student is defined as someone who is 21 years old by 1 October in the year they start their course. Mature students are attractive to both Cambridge and Oxford because they often display a more focused and serious attitude to their studies than younger colleagues. If you are over 21, however, you may prefer to live in a college that admits a large number of mature students (Oxford has one and Cambridge has four of these colleges). The admissions process is the same for mature students as it is for non-mature applicants, and the academic standard required is equally high for both. Naturally, work and life experience are taken into account when considering applications, as well as previous academic qualifications. As with young students, however, it is a good idea to contact a college directly before making your application in order to discuss this issue.

Disabled students

Disabled students are welcome at both universities and are in no way disadvantaged in their application. Disabilities must be declared on the UCAS form in order for the university and college to pool their resources, and you must contact the admissions office at university and college level to discuss your individual needs.

For students with physical disabilities and impaired movement, living in older colleges can be tricky. Because Oxford and Cambridge are so old much of the architecture is 'listed', making it illegal to make changes to the buildings in any way. This means that it is sometimes impossible to install lifts. The same is true of some faculties, for example the architecture faculty at Cambridge. There are, however, many faculties with new buildings, which do not pose such problems, and several colleges in both universities have recently been renovated.

Students with dyslexia are given the opportunity to write using a computer and extra time during exams; they should feel in no way anxious about applying. Those with visual or hearing impairments are also welcome. Each college should have a member of staff responsible for disabled students. You should ring the admissions tutor at your chosen college who will put you in touch with the disability staff member to discuss their resources and your needs. For more information see the links below.

- Cambridge Disability Resource Centre: www.admin.cam.ac.uk/univ/disability/
- Oxford University Disability Advisory Service: www.admin.ox.ac.uk/eop/disab

Students with children

Both Oxford and Cambridge welcome applications from prospective students who have children. Several colleges provide accommodation for couples and families and some colleges have their own nurseries. There is also a university-wide nursery. You should ring the admissions office at your chosen college for more information.

The *Cambridge Guide for Student Parents* is written yearly by the Cambridge University Student Union (CUSU) and is available online at:

www.cusu.cam.ac.uk/welfare/childcare. Some colleges are also members of the Central Childcare Bursary Scheme that makes means-tested grants available to overseas and EU students to help with the costs of childcare. Application forms are available from college offices, the Childcare Information Adviser and CUSU. There are two rounds of applications with closing dates on 1 November and 1 March each year.

Oxford University provides similar support, heavily subsidising the cost of local nursery care, as well as funding holiday play schemes. See www.admin.ox.ac.uk/eop/child/students for further details.

Students from ethnic minorities

It must be said that, to this day, the number of students from ethnic minorities at Oxbridge is low. This has garnered both Oxford and Cambridge a large amount of bad press, perhaps undeservedly. Statistics show that the percentage of minority applicants accepted out of those who apply is very similar to the percentage of white Western applicants who are successful. This suggests that the cause of under-representation of ethnic minorities is primarily due to the lack of applications from these groups, rather than a bias against them, and both universities have outreach policies that aim to attract students from under-represented groups.

Cambridge University states in its Equal Opportunity Policy and Codes of Practice that:

> The University of Cambridge is committed in its pursuit of academic excellence to equality of opportunity and to a pro-active and inclusive approach to equality, which supports and encourages all under-represented groups, promotes an inclusive culture, and values diversity. [The university promises to] monitor the recruitment and progress of all students . . . paying particular attention to the recruitment and progress of ethnic minority students and staff . . .

www.admin.cam.ac.uk/offices/hr/policy/equal

In its Race Equality Policy, Oxford University states that:

> The University of Oxford welcomes diversity amongst its students . . . recognising the contributions to the achievement of the University's mission that can be made by individuals from a wide range of backgrounds and experiences. The University aims to provide an inclusive environment which promotes equality, values diversity and maintains a working, learning and social environment in which the rights and dignity of all its . . . students are respected to assist them in reaching their full potential. The University will work to remove any barriers which might deter people of the highest potential and ability from applying to Oxford, either as staff or students.

www.admin.ox.ac.uk/eop/policy/racepolicy.shtml

Cambridge, in particular, is taking active steps to welcome students from ethnic minorities. The Group to Encourage Ethnic Minority Applications (GEEMA) was recently set up to encourage applications from minority groups, and to explain the application process to students who might otherwise not think of applying. Email geema@cao.cam.ac.uk or telephone: 01223 330873 for more information. Alternatively go to the following address for more information: www.cam.ac.uk/admissions/undergraduate/events/geema.

■ International students

International students are welcome at both Oxford and Cambridge and are valued members of the student population. International students make up less than 10% of the undergraduate population at Cambridge and 14% at Oxford. However, the percentages of overseas students increase at postgraduate level: at Cambridge 50% of postgraduates and at Oxford 63% of postgraduates are international students.

Language requirements

In order to study at Oxford and Cambridge your English must be of a high standard. This is measured by your performance in various different examinations including:

- the IELTS (International English Language Testing System) in which you need a score of at least 7.0 in each section (speaking, listening, writing and reading)
- the English Language GCSE examination at grade B (for Oxford) or C (for Cambridge)
- the TOEFL exam, scoring at least 100
- for EU students, a high grade in English taken as part of a leaving examination (for example the European Baccalaureate and the Abitur) may be acceptable
- an A grade in the Cambridge Certificate in Advanced English or the Cambridge Certificate of Proficiency in English.

The level of English proficiency required depends a great deal on which subject you wish to study. If you want to apply for an essay-based subject (any of the arts or social science subjects including economics, PPE, psychology, history and English language or literature) your written work must be fluent. On the other hand, language is much less important for the study of mathematics. For information about the IELTS exam and where and when it can be taken, visit: www.ielts.org.

Fees

The cost of studying at a UK university for an international student is much higher than for a home student. The tuition fees at Cambridge for the academic year 2009–10 range from £9,747 to £12,768 for most courses although clinical medicine costs £23,631. At Oxford, fees range from £11,750 to £13,450 and for clinical medicine you are asked to pay £24,500. For more information go to the following web addresses.

Cambridge:

- international students: www.cam.ac.uk/admissions/undergraduate/international/
- financial issues for international students: www.cam.ac.uk/admissions/undergraduate/international/finance
- electronic application form: www.cam.ac.uk/admissions/undergraduate/apply/forms/coa

Oxford:

- International Students Information and Advisory Service: www.admin.ox.ac.uk/io/
- official site, including entrance requirements, international qualifications etc: www.ox.ac.uk/admissions/undergraduate_courses/international_students/information_for_international_applicants
- fees for international students: www.admin.ox.ac.uk/studentfunding/fees/
- international student application forms from: www.admissions.ox.ac.uk/forms

Lesbian, gay, bisexual and transsexual (LGBT) students

Oxford and Cambridge are pluralist universities. Not only is there a central LGBT society at each university, but each college also has its own LGBT representative. There are plenty of events to help you feel comfortable. For further information go to the web addresses below.

- **Cambridge:** LesBiGay information from CUSU: www.cusu-lbgt.com
- **Oxford:** LesBiGay at OUSU: www.ousu.org/about/campaigns/a/lgbtq

Educationally disadvantaged students or students who have had a disrupted education

Oxford and Cambridge are committed to helping applicants who have in some way been disadvantaged by a poor school education or by significant disruption to their educational career, which may have resulted in candidates getting lower grades at A level than they might otherwise have achieved.

Cambridge University, in particular, caters for these students with its Cambridge Special Access Scheme (CSAS). On their website, Cambridge states that:

Admissions Tutors are aware that some applicants may not be predicted the high grades required, but will nevertheless have the potential and motivation to follow a course at Cambridge successfully. CSAS . . . is designed to ensure that Colleges have the information they require in order to accurately assess applicants who have experienced particular social or educational disadvantage.

www.cam.ac.uk/admissions/undergraduate/apply/forms/csas

The CSAS is open to UK and EU students only and applicants will be considered if either:

- few people from the applicant's school/college proceed to higher education and the applicant's family has little or no tradition of entry to higher education to study for a degree; or
- the applicant's education has been significantly disrupted or disadvantaged through health or personal problems, disability or difficulties with schooling.

Schools/colleges must complete a CSAS form on behalf of the student in question as individual applications are not considered. For more information, go to www.cam.ac.uk/admissions/undergraduate/apply/forms/csas.

The early stages of preparation

■ Choosing your A level subjects

Usually, if you want to study at Oxford or Cambridge, admissions tutors will expect you to have studied your chosen subject at AS and A level, and to have got a high A grade (at least 90%). This is true of mainstream subjects, such as English, history and mathematics. However, there are some subjects taught at Cambridge and Oxford that do not require you to have taken a previous qualification in the subject.

Subjects that do not require a specific A level include:

- Anglo-Saxon, Norse and Celtic
- archaeology and anthropology
- classical archaeology and ancient history
- classics (Cambridge)
- geography (Cambridge – at Oxford they do want Geography A level)
- history of art
- human sciences
- land economy (Cambridge)
- law
- oriental sciences
- philosophy (Cambridge)
- philosophy and theology
- PPE (Oxford)
- SPS (Cambridge)
- theology.

It is also important to bear in mind that some subjects that are available at A level are not rated highly by Oxford and Cambridge. This is because they feel these subjects do not prepare students for the kind of analytical and problem-solving work expected in higher education. Cambridge even has a list on its website of unacceptable or 'soft' A level subjects that they will not accept.

Cambridge's list of 'soft' A levels includes:

- accounting
- art and design (this may be acceptable in some cases, for example, for fine art at Oxford it is acceptable. Architecture departments may also accept this subject)
- business studies

- communication studies
- dance
- design and technology (this may be acceptable in some cases – check engineering requirements)
- drama/theatre studies (this may be acceptable in some cases – check education and English requirements (Cambridge only))
- film studies
- general studies (as a fourth A level only)
- health and social care
- home economics
- information and communication technology
- leisure studies
- media studies
- music technology
- performance studies
- performing arts
- photography
- physical education
- sports studies
- travel and tourism
- world development.

If you do want to take, or have already taken, one of the above subjects this is not the end of the world as long as you have taken at least three 'hard' subjects that are relevant to your chosen course. In some cases 'soft' subjects may even complement your application. If you wish to study English literature, for example, it could be helpful to study theatre studies as this subject will give you insight into the performative aspects of writing for the stage.

Getting the grades (entry requirements)

Many students apply to Oxford and Cambridge every year on the strength of the reputation of the universities. However, because their fame extends across continents, both universities can afford to be choosy about who they invite to interview. When inviting students to interview, the first thing admissions tutors look at is your exam results. Although the Oxbridge prospectuses generally talk in terms of English qualifications, it should be noted that other school and national examinations, equivalent to English A levels and GCSEs, are equally acceptable. The text below gives details of the qualifications acceptable to Oxford and Cambridge, and the grades that are expected of you at both institutions but for more detailed information about entrance requirements see the following websites.

- **Cambridge:** www.cam.ac.uk/admissions/undergraduate/apply/requirements.html#course
- **Oxford:** www.admissions.ox.ac.uk/int/quals

A levels

If you are taking your exams in England, you should aim to achieve four A grades at AS and A level. You should bear in mind that most students who apply will have, or be predicted, these grades. Universities are now able to see the breakdown of your marks for each subject, and it is expected that you get 100% in at least one module in the subject you wish to continue studying at university.

Whereas Oxford will not be using the new A* grade at A level in their offers for 2010 or 2011, Cambridge welcomes their introduction. An A* will be awarded to students who achieve an A grade overall at A level and also achieve an average of 90% or more on the uniform mark scale (UMS) across their A2 units. The standard A level conditional offer made by the Cambridge colleges for 2010 entry will be A*AA. The subject in which the A* is to be achieved is unlikely to be specified in most cases.

GCSEs

Admissions tutors will also look closely at your GCSE grades. A good applicant will typically have taken 10 or more GCSEs and obtained grades A and A* in all of them.

International Baccalaureate Diploma Programme

Offers are regularly made on the International Baccalaureate at a level of between 7, 6, 6 and 7, 7, 7 in the Higher level subjects, with overall scores between 38 and 42 points out of 45.

Scottish Highers and Advanced Highers

Oxbridge welcome applicants with Scottish qualifications. They do not normally make offers on the basis of Highers alone, and will normally expect applicants to have achieved a minimum of four A grades at Higher grade, plus Advanced Highers. Offers will usually be AAB or AAA in three Advanced Highers. In some cases two Advanced Highers and an additional Higher may be acceptable.

Welsh Baccalaureate

Oxbridge welcome applications from students taking the Advanced Diploma in the Welsh Baccalaureate. Applicants will be expected to have studied three subjects at A level as part of their qualification. Offers will be conditional on achievement in the A levels within the qualification rather than the overall Baccalaureate award.

Irish Leaving Certificate

Applicants from the Republic of Ireland who are studying towards the Irish Leaving Certificate are also welcome to apply. Typical offers for the Irish Leaving Certificate vary from AAAAA to AAABB at Higher level.

Access to HE Diploma

If you are considering applying to Oxbridge as a mature student and are studying an Access to HE Diploma, Oxbridge require 60 credits with a minimum of 45 credits at level 3 (or equivalent). Applicants may be required to meet additional subject-specific requirements for particular courses at Cambridge. Details of these additional requirements are listed at: www.cam.ac.uk/admissions/undergraduate/apply/requirements.html#alevel. For further information you may contact the FE Access Officer in the Cambridge Admissions Office (tel: 01223 765728; email: feaccess@cao.cam.ac.uk) or the admissions staff in one of the Cambridge colleges.

European Baccalaureate

If you are studying towards the European Baccalaureate, note that successful applicants are typically asked for 85% overall with 90% in those subjects that relate most closely to the course they wish to study.

French Baccalaureate

Typical offers for applicants taking the French Baccalaureate are 16 or 17 ('mention très bien') out of 20. Applicants are also usually asked to achieve 16 or 17 in specific subjects.

German Abitur

If you are studying towards the German Abitur, note that applicants are typically asked for an overall score of between 1.0 and 1.3, with 13 or 14 in those subjects that relate most closely to the course they wish to study.

Cambridge Pre-U

Cambridge Pre-U is a post-16 qualification designed to prepare students with the skills important at university. It challenges students to show not only a keen grasp of their subject, but also lateral, critical and contextual thinking. It encourages independent research and promotes learning through innovative approaches to the curriculum and assessment. Both universities will accept the Pre-U but express no preference for it over any other qualification.

The extended project

The extended project is a separate qualification that A level students may add to their study programme. Students carry out a project on a topic of their choosing which may or may not be linked to their chosen A level subjects. The projects involve planning, research and evaluation, but the end product may be in the form of a dissertation, a performance or an artefact. The aim of the extended project is to develop research and independent learning skills that will be of great benefit in higher education and employment. Currently neither university uses the extended project in its offers, but they recognise the benefits: the skills which can ease the transition from secondary to higher education. Cambridge has stated that the extended project may be a suitable topic for discussion at interview and in some cases, where it is relevant, it may be an appropriate piece of written work to be submitted.

The Diploma

The specialised Diploma for 14–19-year-olds has been created to provide an alternative to more traditional qualifications. Both Oxford and Cambridge will accept the Advanced Diploma in Engineering for applicants to their engineering courses. However, applicants for engineering will also need A level Physics and the level 3 Certificate in Mathematics. Neither university has made any statement as to their acceptance of other Diploma subjects.

Cambridge Special Access Scheme

If, for health reasons, or because your school has not given you the support you need to reach your potential in exams, students from the UK and EU may apply, via their school, for the Cambridge Special Access Scheme (see Chapter 1, pages 11–12).

▉ Gap years

Policies about taking gap years vary from college to college, and from subject to subject, so it is important that you discuss your plans with the admissions tutor at your chosen college well in advance of your application. If you want to study a subject where languages are helpful (art history, history, music and modern languages to name only four), then taking a gap year to improve your fluency in a second or third language may give you a distinct advantage. On the other hand, if you are applying for maths, admissions tutors may be afraid that you will forget your A level knowledge during the year out and be reluctant to accept you. If you do decide to take a gap year it is absolutely essential that you make concrete and creative plans. Admissions tutors will want to see proof of your experiences in your Personal Statement and at interview, and will expect your time to have been spent constructively, in a way that will enhance your university studies.

You also need to decide whether to make an application for deferred entry (this is when you apply whilst doing your A levels, two years in advance of your first term at university) or to apply a year after your school friends do, whilst you are on your year out. When making this decision you should ring your college of choice to discuss their preferences. Some Cambridge and Oxford colleges do not like making offers to deferred entrants, simply because this means they have to commit a place before they have met competing applicants for the following year. In this case, colleges encourage you to wait a year and apply whilst on your gap year. If you ask their advice and make the most of your time out, you can guarantee that you will not be penalised. In allowing yourself time to mature, you may even make a better application and become a more attractive candidate.

As the Cambridge prospectus explains:

> About one in five students coming to Cambridge take a gap year before starting their studies. This year out proves a very useful time in which to improve skills, earn money, travel and generally gain maturity and self-reliance.

Cambridge Prospectus, 2008–9

◼ How to make your application shine: work experience

Work experience can be a great way to explore the subject you hope to study at university. Experience within the work environment is particularly important if you want to study a vocational subject, for example law or medicine. It is often only in a work situation that one can fully understand the stresses, responsibilities and pleasures that go along with a particular career, and only then can you really commit. Work experience can provide admissions tutors with strong evidence that candidates are committed, determined and have thought their applications through carefully. It can also provide you with a goal that keeps you motivated even through the toughest periods of study.

Apart from having a real idea of where you might end up in five years time, work experience can expose you to ideas related to the subject you are about to study in exciting ways. For example, if you want to study natural sciences at Cambridge, try to get a week during school holidays helping or observing at a laboratory where the scientists are working on something you are particularly interested in. You will be able to sit in on lab meetings and hear for yourself the problems that they face and the solutions they come to. You can also ask them personally for reading suggestions. No one will be as ahead of the game as they will, and this will give you some really exciting things to discuss at interview.

Above are only three examples of subjects where work experience is helpful but this is applicable to any subject. If you are really serious about studying and learning, find a way to get more information within the work environment. This will not only give you greater knowledge and confidence, it will also show the admissions tutors that you are really interested. Remember, however, work experience should be directly relevant to your chosen subject.

Organising work experience can take several months; patience and persistence are necessary, particularly in the economic climate of today. Statistically, the most successful method of finding these placements – indeed in finding jobs after university – is through networking: asking friends and family. Tell everyone you know what you are planning to do at university and what you are particularly interested in, and ask if they know anyone who might give you a hand. Second, target institutions, departments and companies directly. If you have a contact there, ring him or her, otherwise ring the HR department. Do ring, don't just send them a letter asking for help, since people are more likely to remember your voice than an envelope or email. Once you have spoken to some-one in person, tell them you are going to send them a follow-up email with your CV and a cover letter. Write the email and send it immediately. Then ring them back a few days later to ask whether they have received your letter and email, and whether they have any task to give you.

> *I wanted to get some work experience in the media business but had no contacts. I wrote letters to 15 organisations 'cold'. Ten never got back to me, four were unable to take me on as they had other work experience students and one offered me a week's work experience. I would definitely apply to many organisations at the same time.*

Oxford Applicant

Sample letters for work experience

Below is a sample letter you could send to gain some work experience. The words in italics need to be adapted as appropriate for your situation.

Mr Joe Bloggs MP   Your address
The House of Commons   Your telephone number
Westminster   Your email address
London SW1
Date

Dear Mr Bloggs,

I would very much like to *undertake some work experience in your office/shadow you for a week* because I am very interested in exploring a career in *politics*. I am currently studying for *my A levels in Spanish, Maths and Chemistry* at *Green Fields School* and I have enclosed/attached my CV for your kind consideration. My summer holiday starts on *14th July* and continues until *16th August*, and I would be so grateful if there was any time between these two dates when I could come in. Please could you contact me at the address or email above at your convenience. I look forward to hearing from you.

Yours sincerely,

Your signature

Your name

Enc. CV

There are some important points to note here.

■ If you know the name of the person to whom you are writing a cover letter, you need to sign off 'Yours sincerely'. If you do not know the name of the person, you write 'Dear Sir/Madam' or 'To whom it may concern', and sign off 'Yours faithfully'.

■ It is much better to write the person's name rather than write a generic 'To whom it may concern', so make a phone call and find out who deals with work experience or who the Human Resources Manager is. If you are writing a letter to a contact, then address the letter directly to them.

■ Whether you ask for work experience or to shadow someone depends on their profession. If they are a barrister or a doctor it would be best to shadow them, which means following them throughout the week and attending everything they attend. If you are applying to work in a business then you should ask for work experience as you could be given a project to do and really demonstrate your skills (which you can then write about in your Personal Statement).

■ It is important to organise your work experience well in advance (at least three months) as businesses and organisations are inundated with requests for work experience.

■ Although it is more efficient to email your work experience letter and CV, you should also send a hard copy. It has been proven that this is more memorable to employers than emailed versions.

■ If you do not hear back after a week to 10 days, you should email them again and telephone them. Make absolutely sure they have received your documents.

■ On the last day of your work experience, hand in a thank-you letter, using the model letter below, and ask if they are happy to write a reference to send to your teacher. This is crucial as your teacher can then incorporate comments in their UCAS reference about your experience. An example of a reference from an employer is given on the next page.

Mr Joe Bloggs MP
The House of Commons
Westminster
London SW1
Date

Your address
Your telephone number
Your email address

Dear Mr Bloggs,

Thank you so much for *showing me around the House of Commons on Tuesday*, and for letting me *work in your office this week*. I really enjoyed it – *especially being allowed to watch the House of Commons debate*. I was wondering if you would be so kind as to write a short reference about me and send it to my teacher at *Green Fields School, Ealing London, WO 0AA*.

Thank you very much again.

Yours sincerely

Your signature

Your name

Sample curriculum vitae (CV) for work experience

At this stage of your life, you may feel that there is little to write on your CV. However, the CV is a useful document to enclose with your work experience letter as it gives the employer some useful basic information about you.

The format of CVs varies considerably, but a general rule of thumb is that they must not exceed two A4 pages in length, they must be word processed and not handwritten and they must be easy to read.

You must be able to back up anything you write on your CV, just like your Personal Statement. Put down any work experience you have, including babysitting, as your employer may want a reference for you. If you have absolutely no work experience, you could ask your teacher to write a reference for you. You should regularly update your CV. You will find that when you come to apply for jobs after university, your work experience will still be very useful. These model letters can be used when you are applying for internships in your summer holidays too.

JOSEPHINE SMITH

Your address
Tel: 01234 567890
Mobile: 07777 123 456
Email: myemail@email.com

Nationality: British
Date of Birth: 7 February 1990

EDUCATION

Green Fields School, London (2001–08)

3 A levels (Grades pending)
Spanish, Chemistry, Maths

10 GCSEs

Grade A*: French, Latin, Spanish, Dual Award Science, English Language, English Literature, History, Computer Studies
Grade A: Mathematics

SKILLS

Presentation

- Can explain ideas clearly and concisely (presentations at school)
- Excellent public-speaking skills (debated competitively for school)
- Inter-personal skills
- Negotiation and organisational skills (founded and chaired charity committee)

Analysis

- Won a prize for ICT GCSE project write-up which tested a system I devised
- Research and writing
- Commended for research and writing skills in Spanish essay

Computation

- Skilled in Microsoft Word, Excel, Internet Explorer, Power Point

WORK EXPERIENCE

Babysitting; July 2007
Newspaper round, Green Field newsagent, London; January 2006–January 2007

INTERESTS AND ACTIVITIES

- Part of the netball team
- Enjoy cooking
- Enjoy going to the theatre

Example of an employer reference from shadowing a professional

Georgina spent a week with us at the National Hospital for Neurology on a work placement. During that time she closely observed the work of physicians, surgeons and nurses as they cared for people whilst inpatients and outpatients. Georgina is clearly committed to a career in medicine and has an advanced and realistic understanding of its demands. Our impression was that Georgina as well as being very academic has excellent empathetic and social skills. She was very enthusiastic about the time she spent with us and will make an excellent doctor. She was at all times punctual and reliable and her pleasant manner both with staff and patients was of specific note. Her interest, enthusiasm and intelligence bode well for her as she follows her desired path of interest in medicine. I have no hesitation in recommending her for placement in medical school.

Example of an employer reference from volunteering over a sustained period of time

Georgina has volunteered at the Hospice for a year and is a most valuable member of the team of volunteers. She is dedicated and committed, doing regular shifts here. Georgina has been very dependable and reliable, proving that she can handle awkward and sometimes potentially upsetting situations with great tact and maturity.

Despite having a busy study schedule Georgina has volunteered her own precious spare time at weekends – and given invaluable service to the Hospice. It is always a pleasure to see her and her enthusiasm is infectious.

Georgina is very popular with members of staff and other volunteers alike. Patients, who in many instances are extremely ill, especially appreciate seeing a friendly and familiar face.

Both these references would both be very helpful to your teacher in writing your reference, as they help to explain how you behave in a non-academic environment.

Events in your area

Even if you have done some relevant work experience, you should be constantly on the look-out for events in your area that are relevant to the subject that you want to study. Local libraries often host talks by renowned authors, the Royal Institute and the Science Museum in London host regular science lectures, the Royal Geographic Society organises regular discussions with eminent geographers and the Royal Academy of Art has an ongoing art history lecture series. In addition, the universities in your area may hold lectures that could interest you. Speak to your teachers for ideas or go online to search for relevant events.

Ideas you might consider include:

- politics: go on a tour of the Houses of Parliament
- law: sit in the public gallery of your local magistrate's or Crown Court
- history and archaeology: visit the British Museum
- art and history of art: visit every gallery and museum you can get to, including the galleries local to Oxford and Cambridge.

You should also be constantly on the look-out for news stories that relate to developments in your field. Try to get as big a picture as possible about your subject: about how it relates to the rest of the word and why it might be important to know about.

Making a first class application
UCAS and preparation before the interview

Choosing the right university

Deciding between Cambridge and Oxford may seem daunting, and you cannot apply to both. Most students have a gut feeling about where they want to go. You may have visited the cities as a tourist and found one more attractive than the other. You may also have gone to an open day at both universities and found one more friendly or welcoming. These are all perfectly good reasons for making your choice. If, however, you are still in a quandary, the following information may give you some help.

Choosing the university by subject is one way of simplifying matters. It is essential to check that the university you prefer teaches the subject you wish to study. There are various subjects that Oxford offers which Cambridge does not and vice versa.

Subjects you can study at Cambridge but not at Oxford include:

- architecture
- economics (as a stand-alone subject; in Oxford you do a combined course of economics and management)
- education studies
- land economy
- the languages Dutch, Anglo-Saxon, Norse and Celtic
- management studies (as a stand-alone subject; in Oxford you do a combined course of economics and management)
- natural sciences (at Oxford all the sciences are offered but not in the same combination)
- philosophy (as a stand-alone subject; at Oxford you do a combined course of philosophy, politics and economics)
- social and political science (SPS)
- veterinary medicine.

Subjects you can study at Oxford but not at Cambridge include:

- the languages Sanskrit and Czech with Slovak
- philosophy, politics and economics (PPE)

- psychology, philosophy and physiology (PPP)
- separate sciences (although you do have to take modules in other science subjects as well).

Subjects you can study at both universities include:

- archaeology and anthropology
- classics
- computer science
- engineering
- English literature and language
- geography
- history
- human sciences
- law
- modern and medieval languages
- music
- Oriental studies (at Oxford) and Asian and Middle Eastern studies (at Cambridge)
- theology and religious studies.

It is important to note that, although many subjects are the same, their components may differ between the two universities, and you should take time to compare the courses in detail.

For more information go to the websites listed below.

- **Cambridge:** www.cam.ac.uk/admissions/undergraduate
- **Oxford:** www.admissions.ox.ac.uk

Differences in course structure at Oxford and Cambridge

Comparing the Tripos system at Cambridge with the two-part system at Oxford can be another way to help you to decide which university is better suited to you. One of the great attractions of Cambridge is the flexibility of its Tripos system (the name Tripos is said to have been derived from the three-legged stool that undergraduates in the Middle Ages sat on for their oral examinations).

Each course, or Tripos, is usually divided into two parts: Part I and Part II. After each 'part' there is an exam that counts towards your final undergraduate mark. A 'Part I' can take one year (in economics, for example) or two years (in English). A two-year Part I is divided into Part IA and Part IB. Once you have completed Part I (A and B), you have the option of either continuing to specialise in the same subject, or swapping to a related but different subject for Part II.

In theory this gives students quite a bit of flexibility, and there have been students who have studied three different related subjects during the course of their three years at Cambridge and come out with a First Class degree. In reality, however, you should not go to interview thinking that you will be able to change courses easily.

Admissions tutors, particularly those interviewing for humanities, arts and social sciences, will see this as a sign that a student is not committed to their subject, and give the place to someone who is. If students want to change subject when they get to Cambridge they have to work very hard at convincing their existing DOS that they want to change for the right reasons. Then students have to convince a DOS in their new subject to take them on.

On the other hand there are subjects where elongated undergraduate degrees are encouraged. Natural science and mathematics students have the option of adding a Part III, while engineering students take Parts IA, IB, IIA and IIB over four years, leading ultimately to the award of MEng.

The system works slightly differently at Oxford. As in Cambridge, students have to pass exams in two parts. However, students do not have to take examinations at the end of each year, as is the case in many Cambridge courses. The Preliminary Examinations (or 'Prelims') are taken at the end of the first year (except for experimental psychology and PPP, where they are taken at the end of the second term), and the Final Examinations ('Finals') are taken at the end of the third year. So most undergraduates at Oxford University do not take exams in their second year.

In general there are more courses at Oxford which are designed to take four years. The joint honours courses of mathematics and philosophy and physics and philosophy, as well as classics, take four years. Mathematics itself, physics and earth sciences can take either three or four years (your choice), but in the case of molecular and cellular biochemistry, chemistry, engineering and metallurgy, students are normally expected to progress to the fourth research-based year leading to the award of the master's degree.

You should research the similarities and differences as they apply to your particular subject choice carefully, and then be prepared to discuss your discoveries when it comes to interview.

■ Choosing the right college or making an open application

Oxford has 30 colleges and six permanent private halls and Cambridge has 29 colleges, so there is a lot of choice. Remember that your college is the place where you will be living, every day, probably for the next three years, so it is absolutely essential to choose a place where you feel comfortable.

The obvious way to get an immediate feel for a college is to visit it. Have a wander round, talk to the porters at the front gate and let them know that you are thinking of applying. They will have many stories to tell. Alternatively you can visit the colleges on an official open day, where you can meet other applicants and some of the college fellows. For information about open days go to the websites below.

- **Cambridge:** www.cam.ac.uk/admissions/undergraduate/opendays
- **Oxford:** www.ox.ac.uk/admissions/undergraduate_courses/open_days

Another way to find out about a college is to pick up the phone and have a chat with the admissions tutor. If he or she sounds friendly and welcoming it is a sure sign that you will be made to feel at home.

To get the telephone numbers of different colleges and to get more information, look at the university prospectuses as well as the individual college prospectuses. These can also be downloaded online at the addresses below.

- **Cambridge:** www.cam.ac.uk/admissions/undergraduate/ publications/prospectus
- **Oxford:** www.ox.ac.uk/admissions/prospectuses

In addition, each Junior Common Room (JCR) also produces a student-written 'alternative prospectus'; this is less formal and gives you the student perspective on the college. Again, contact the college or ask for the email of the JCR president to order a copy. All prospectuses will be sent to you free of charge. You can also download these alternative prospectuses from the addresses below.

- **Cambridge:** www.cusu.cam.ac.uk/prospective/prospectus
- **Oxford:** www.ousu.org/prospective-students

Whilst you visit the colleges and read the prospectuses, there are a number of factors that you should consider in order to make a good college choice. Some of these factors are academic, others are personal, and both are equally important. Make sure you consider the points below.

- Whether the college offers your subject. Not all colleges offer every subject, so this is the first thing to find out. Oxford produces a table that summarises this information at www.admissions.ox.ac.uk/ colleges/availab. For Cambridge you will have to look at each college separately.
- Who your tutor or DOS is likely to be. As mentioned previously, an academic from a particular faculty will also be a 'fellow' of a college. The fellow at your college is likely to be your tutor or DOS, and will probably be your interviewer. It is, therefore, a good idea to know where his/her particular interests lie. Although, at undergraduate level, your work will probably be faculty based, it is always an added bonus if the academic at your college has done research in an area

you find fascinating. This is, in any event, a reason for college choice that you can mention at interview. You can find out who the fellows are at your college (and in your subject) by going to your faculty website, where the members of staff will be listed alongside their college and research interests.

- The size of the college. Small colleges often feel more cosy and you are more likely to know all your peers. In large colleges you will feel more anonymous but will have a wealth of new people to meet.
- The distance from the college to the centre of town and your faculty. It is often overlooked, but a 20-minute cycle ride from college to a faculty lecture in the pouring rain can be extremely unpleasant. On the other hand, colleges further from the centre tend to have larger grounds for sport, and more of a communal atmosphere.
- Whether the college offers accommodation for the duration of your studies. Some colleges only provide accommodation for the first year and you are expected to find a house after that. Some people like living in a house with their friends but there are associated problems, for example unhelpful landlords and houses that are far away from your college.
- Whether the college is modern or old. You may feel more at home in a newly renovated suite than a older room with 'character'.
- The size and facilities of the accommodation available. Most college accommodation consists of a single room, perhaps with an en-suite bathroom, but more usually shared bathrooms on one staircase. Some colleges have gyms, some have practice rooms for musicians, some have neither.
- The politics of entrance. The ratio of students who come from state or private schools, between men and women and between traditional entrants and ethnic minorities differ from college to college. These figures are given on each college's prospectus. You may need to take into consideration the political leanings of a college. Some colleges are very left wing (King's College, Cambridge, for example) and accept less than average numbers of privately schooled applicants. Others are happy to accept students from private schools. The reputation of a college is worth researching for this reason.

The Norrington and Tompkins tables

Another way to choose a college is by looking at where it comes in the league tables. These rank colleges according to their undergraduates' success in their final exams. At Oxford the league table is called the Norrington Table (Table 1) and in Cambridge it is called the Tompkins Table (Table 2). Degrees obtained at the college are scored in the following way: five points for a First; three for a 2:1; two for a 2:2 and one for a Third. The scores shown in Tables 1 and 2 are the percentages of total points available.

Table 1: College undergraduate degree classifications 2008/09 (sorted by rank)

College	Score	Rank
St John's	76.51%	1
Merton	76.43%	2
Magdalen	76.04%	3
Corpus Christi	73.55%	4
New	72.92%	5
Hertford	72.80%	6
University	72.24%	7
Lincoln	71.69%	8
Wadham	71.50%	9
Queen's	71.49%	10
Trinity	71.14%	11
Christ Church	70.64%	12
Keble	70.58%	13
Balliol	70.26%	14
Worcester	70.25%	15
St Catherine's	69.76%	16
Jesus	69.68%	17
Exeter	69.39%	18
Somerville	68.82%	19
St Anne's	68.50%	20
Lady Margaret Hall	67.84%	21
St Hugh's	67.79%	22
Pembroke	67.75%	23
Oriel	67.37%	24
St Peter's	67.06%	25
Brasenose	66.48%	26
St Edmund Hall	65.44%	27
Mansfield	65.25%	28
St Hilda's	61.51%	29
Harris Manchester	59.23%	30

Source: www.ox.ac.uk/about_the_university/facts_and_figures/undergraduate_ degr_1.html These rankings should be treated with caution, since the number of degrees awarded per college is small, and the results are dependent on the performance of a particular group of students in a particular year. The University of Oxford does not recommend that students base their college choice on such rankings.

Table 2: Tompkins table 2009

Rank*	College	Score	% Firsts
1 (3)	Trinity	68.83%	33.40%
2 (2)	Emmanuel	66.99%	26.20%
3 (1)	Selwyn	66.91%	26.80%
4 (4)	Gonville & Caius	66.85%	26.30%
5 (11)	St Catharine's	66.58%	27.10%
6 (10)	Pembroke	66.00%	28.10%
7 (6)	Churchill	65.48%	25.40%
8 (5)	Magdalene	65.35%	23.30%
9 (15)	Trinity Hall	65.03%	22.90%
10 (9)	Corpus Christi	64.88%	22.00%
11 (7)	Jesus	64.81%	21.50%
12 (16)	Queens'	64.08%	23.10%
13 (8)	Christ's	63.88%	23.20%
14 (20)	St John's	63.51%	21.20%
15 (12)	Downing	63.44%	19.70%
16 (17)	Peterhouse	62.99%	23.60%
17 (19)	King's	62.24%	20.20%
18 (13)	Clare	62.18%	19.70%
19 (18)	Robinson	62.16%	20.10%
20 (22)	Girton	61.80%	17.30%
21 (21)	Fitzwilliam	61.23%	18.30%
22 (14)	Sidney Sussex	60.75%	14.40%
23 (23)	New Hall	60.30%	15.70%
24 (24)	Newnham	58.98%	12.20%
25 (25)	Homerton	58.25%	13.10%
26 (26)	Hughes Hall	56.30%	16.70%
27 (27)	Wolfson	55.03%	7.90%
28 (29)	St Edmund's	52.96%	9.40%
29 (28)	Lucy Cavendish	52.90%	6.70%

* 2008 rank shown in brackets
Source: The *Independent*

Open applications

If you are still unsure about which college is for you, there is the option of making an open application. This is an application where you do not specify a college on your UCAS form; instead, the admissions computer will assign you to a college that is undersubscribed in your subject. Approximately 15% of students applying to Oxbridge make open applications, and the success rates are the same as for college-specific applications. Obviously, if there is a college that you really do not want to go to it is a bad idea to apply in this way, since you may be assigned to the very college you want to avoid. However, an open application may be a good way to settle your doubts, and most students end up loving their college, even if it was not their first choice. The following two statements made by admissions tutors from Oxford and Cambridge may help to put your mind at rest.

If an applicant makes an open application and the statistical programme allocates that candidate to our college, the candidate will be treated as if they applied directly to our college.

Admissions Tutor, Cambridge

Cooperative arrangements between the colleges are designed to ensure that able candidates applying to oversubscribed college are placed at other colleges. Almost 20% of successful candidates are placed at a college other than their college of preference each year.

Oxford Prospectus, 2009

◼ Choosing the right course

Choosing the right course for you is possibly the most important decision you will have to make during the whole application process. It is primarily your enthusiasm for your subject that will be attractive to the admissions tutors and interviewers. Remember that the academics who teach at Oxford and Cambridge, and who interview prospective students, have dedicated their whole lives to their subject. They believe passionately in the importance of their research and expect you to do the same. In addition, if you get accepted, the vast majority of your time as an undergraduate will be spent working. There is probably more responsibility and expectation placed on students at Oxbridge than any other university in the UK. Good students at Oxford and Cambridge will typically work for 12 hours per day – sometimes more during exam term. Whereas students in an essay-based course at UCL, for example, will be asked to write four 2,500 word essays over the course of a 10-week term, Oxbridge students are asked to write between 12 and 14 essays of the same length in the course of an eight-week term. The more excited you are by this work, the more likely your experience will be tolerable and worthwhile.

In order to make the right choice it is important to gather as much information about a course and its content as possible. Prospectuses for Oxford and Cambridge give detailed course guides, including information on course content and A level requirements. In addition, Oxford makes individual prospectuses for each subject. Read this information and the criteria very carefully, making sure your qualifications fulfil the requirements specified.

If you want to be really thorough, contact the individual faculty secretaries at each university. Remember that, while the college administers the teaching, it is the faculty (i.e. the subject department within the university) that controls the syllabus. The faculty secretary will have much more detail on course content than is available in the prospectuses. Information about faculty addresses, including website addresses, is available in the prospectuses; Cambridge applicants may also refer to *The Cambridge University Guide to Courses*, published by Cambridge University Press.

When you talk with the faculty secretary, ask him or her for an up-to-date reading list for new undergraduates. This will list the books that students are expected to read before they come up to Cambridge or Oxford for the first time. If you dip into some of these books you will get an idea of the sort of information you will be tackling if you study the subject. In addition, if you have time to visit Cambridge or Oxford again, you could spend the afternoon in the university bookshop (Blackwell's in Oxford or Heffer's in Cambridge). The staff at both bookshops are very familiar with the texts used by undergraduates. Of course, if you know any current undergraduates at either university, discuss their work with them.

Collecting this information will boost your confidence and reassure you about your subject decision. Remember, in order to argue your case at interview, and to cope with the workload if you get a place, you must be deeply committed to your subject.

Recommended reading and films

Following is a list of suggested books and films that may help you to start your research into your chosen subject. It is not exhaustive or essential reading, but will give you some direction.

Economics/management

- *The Long Tail*, Chris Anderson
- *The Corporation*, Joel Bakan
- *Poor Story (Globalisation)*, Giles Bolton
- *Good to Great*, Jim Collins
- *Myself and Other Important Matters*, Charles Handy
- *The Undercover Economist*, Tim Harford

- *The Writing on the Wall: China and the West in the 21st Century*, Will Hutton
- *China Shakes the World*, James Kynge
- *How They Started*, David Lester
- *Freakonomics*, S Levitt and S Dubner
- *The Starbucks Experience*, Joseph Michelli
- *Confessions of an Economic Hit Man*, John Perkins
- *Capitalism*, Jonathan Porritt
- *How Rich Countries Got Rich*, Eric S Reinhart
- *The Dragon and the Elephant (India and China)*, David Smith
- *Globalisation and its Discontents*, Joseph Stiglitz
- *Making Globalisation Work*, Joseph Stiglitz
- *Fooled By Randomness*, Nasim Nicholas Talib
- *Swimming Against the Stream*, Tim Waterstone
- *The Google Story*, David A Wise

English

If you have a favourite author or authors and you mention them in your Personal Statement, be sure to have read as much of their work as possible. Know your author as well as their works. Investigate them as people, rather than only appreciating their writing. In addition, the following books are interesting works.

- *Beginning Theory: An introduction to Literary and Cultural Theory*, Peter Barry
- *The Soul of the Age: Life, Mind and World of William Shakespeare*, Jonathan Bate
- *Literary Theory: A Very Short Introduction*, Jonathan Culler
- *On Deconstruction: Theory and Criticism after Structuralism*, Jonathan Culler
- *Structuralist Poetics*, Jonathan Culler
- *Critical Approaches to English Literature*, David Daiches
- *Literary Theory: An Introduction*, Terry Eagleton
- *Revenge Tragedy: From Aeschylus to Armageddon*, John Kerrigan
- *Shakespeare The Thinker*, A D Nuttall
- *Why Does Tragedy Give Pleasure?*, A D Nuttall

History

The key piece of advice for would-be Oxbridge historians is to ensure that you have read widely around your A level topics. You need to show an awareness of recent historical debate and to understand different interpretations of the same events. The books listed below either deal with historiography or are particularly well written and deserve attention:

- *Pursuit of Glory*, Tim Blanning
- *The Historian's Craft*, Marc Bloch
- *History and Social Theory*, Peter Burke
- *In Churchill's Shadow*, David Cannadine
- *What is History?*, E H Carr

- *The Practice of History*, Geoffrey Elton
- *In Defence of History*, Richard J Evans
- *Dark Continent: Europe's Twentieth Century*, Mark Mazower
- *The Pursuit of History*, John Tosh
- *Roundhead Reputations*, Blair Worden

Law

- *The Law Machine*, Marcel Berlins and Clare Dyer
- *The Discipline of Law*, Lord Denning
- *The Politics of the Judiciary*, J A G Griffith
- *The Juryman's Tale*, Trevor Grove
- *The Magistrate's Tale*, Trevor Grove
- *The New Penguin Guide to the Law*, John Pritchard
- *McLibel: Burger Culture on Trial*, John Vidal
- *Learning the Law*, Glanville Williams

Medicine

- *Stop the 21st Century Killing You*, Dr Paula Bailie-Hamilton
- *Catching Cold*, Pete Davies and Michael Joseph
- *The Human Brain: A Guided Tour*, Susan Greenfield
- *Aspirin*, Diarmuid Jeffreys
- *The Trouble with Medicine*, Dr Melvin Konner
- *How We Die*, Sherwin Nuland
- *How We Live*, Sherwin Nuland
- *Don't Die Young*, Dr Alice Roberts
- *Everything You Need to Know about Bird Flu*, Jo Revill
- *Practical Medical Ethics*, David Seedhouse and Lisetta Lovett
- *Body Story*, Dr David Wilham

Modern languages
French: reading

- *La Chute*, Camus
- *La Clé sur la Porte*, Marie Cardinal
- *Trois Contes*, Flaubert
- *La Porté troite*, A Gide
- *Le Misanthrope*, Molière
- *Sur la Lecture*, Proust
- *Maximes*, La Rochefoucauld
- *Candide ou Micromegas [très court]*, Voltaire

French: films

Truffaut, Robert Bresson, André Téchiné, Eric Rohmer and Louis Malle [ses *le films français*] are important figures. Read the following texts if possible:

- *Les films de ma vie*, Truffaut
- *Notes sur le cinématographe*, Bresson

German: reading

- *Die Verlorene Ehre der Katharina Blum*, Heinrich Böll
- *Kaukasischer Kreidekreis; Mutter Courage*, Bertolt Brecht
- *Die Physiker; Der Besuch der alten Dame*, Friedrich Dürrenmatt
- *Ideology of the Aesthetic; Literary theory*, Terry Eagleton (for articles on psychoanalytic literary theory)
- *Andorra*, Max Frisch
- *Die Blechtrommel; Katz und Maus*, Gunther Grass
- *Die Verwandlung; Sämtliche Erzählungen*, Franz Kafka
- *Tonio Kröger; Der Tod in Venedig*, Thomas Mann
- *Der Vorleser*, Bernhard Schlink (the book not the film!)
- *Das Parfum; Die Taube*, Patrick Süskind

German: art

Taschen books are easily available and cheap. Read in English or German.

- Expressionism
- Bauhaus
- Wiener Werkstätte

German: films

Films about the Second World War:

- *Das Boot*
- *Europa, Europa*
- *Die Faelscher*
- *Heimat*
- *Sophie Scholl*
- *Der Untergang*

Films about the former East Germany:

- *Goodbye Lenin!*
- *Der Himmel über Berlin*
- *Leben der Anderen*
- *Sonnenallee*
- *Der Tunnel*

General films:

- *Alice in den Städten*
- *The American Friend*
- *Angst essen Seele auf*
- *Die Apothekerin*
- *Die Ehe der Maria Braun*
- *Das Experiment*
- *Gegen die Wand*
- *Lola Rennt*
- *Napola*

Italian: reading

- *Se una notte d'inverno un viaggiatore*, Italo Calvino
- *Lessico famigliare*, Natalia Ginzburg
- *Il gattopardo*, Tomasi di Lampedusa
- *Se questo è un uomo*, Primo Levi
- *Sei personaggi in cerca d'autore*, Pirandello
- *A ciascuno il suo*, Leonardo Sciascia
- *La coscienza di Zeno*, Italo Svevo

Russian: reading

- *Requiem*, Anna Akhmatova
- *Collected Poems in English 1972–1999*, Iosif Brodsky
- *The Master and Margarita*, Mikhail Bulgakov
- *Life of Arseniev*, Ivan Bunin
- *Uncle Vanya*, Anton Chekhov
- *The Brothers Karamazov*, Fyodor Dostoevsky
- *Taras Bul'ba*, Nikolai Gogol
- *A Hero of our Time*, Mikhail Lermontov
- *Doctor Zhivago*, Boris Pasternak
- *Eugene Onegin*, Alexander Pushkin
- *One Day in the Life of Ivan Denisovich*, Aleksandr Solzhenitsyn
- *Anna Karenina*, Lev Tolstoy
- *A Month in the Country*, Ivan Turgenev

Spanish: reading

- *La Regenta*, Leopoldo Alas
- *La Vida es Sueño*, Pedro Calderón de la Barca
- *El Árbol de la Ciencia*, Pio Baroja
- *La Familia de Pascual Duarte; La Colmena*, Camilo José Cela
- *El Quijote*, Miguel de Cervantes
- *Rayuela*, Julio Cortázar
- *Cinco Horas con Mario*, Miguel Delibes
- *El Jarama*, Rafael Sánchez Ferlosio
- *Lo Raro es Vivir*, Carmen Martin Gaite
- *Señas de identidad*, Juan Goytisolo
- *La Ciudad y los Perros*, Mario Vargas Llosa
- *Poeta en Nueva York; La Casa de Bernarda Alba*, Federico García Lorca
- *El Surrealismo y Cuatro Poetas de la Generación del 27: (Ensayo Sobre Extensión y Límites Del Surrealismo en la Generación Del 27)*, Carlos Marcial
- *Corazón Tan Blanco*, Javier Marías
- *Cien Años de Soledad*, Gabriel Garciúa Márquez
- *Tiempo de Silencio*, Luis Martin-Santos
- *Olvidado Rey Gudú*, Ana María Matute
- *La Ciudad de los Prodigios*, Eduardo Mendoza

- *Confieso Que he Vivido*, Pablo Neruda
- *La Celestina*, Fernando de Rojas
- *La Tía Tula*, Miguel de Unamuno

Spannish: films

- *Todo Sobre mi Madre*, Pedro Almodóvar
- *Las Bicicletas son Para el Verano*, Jaime Chávarri
- *El Espíritu de la Colmena*, Víctor Erice
- *Amores Perros*, Alejandro González Iñárritu
- *La Caza; Cría Cuervos; Elisa, Vida Mía*, Carlos Saura

Psychology

- *Mapping the Mind*, Rita Carter
- *Totem and Talent*, Sigmund Freud
- *Emotional Intelligence*, Daniel Goleman
- *Body Language*, Allan Pease
- *Memory*, David Samuel
- *Phobias – Fighting the Fear*, Helen Saul
- *The Human Mind*, Robert Winston

Science/engineering/maths

- Any book by Einstein
- *Genesis Machines*, Martyn Amos
- *Critical Mass*, Philip Ball
- *The Infinite Book*, John D Barrow
- *How Long is a Piece of String?*, Rob Eastaway and Jeremy Wyndham
- *Chaos*, James Glick
- *The Elegant Universe*, Brian Greene
- *The Equation that couldn't be solved*, Mario Livio
- *Black Bodies and Quantum Cats*, Jennifer Ouellette
- *Dr Riemann's Zeros*, Karl Sabbagh
- *Zero*, Charles Seife
- *Fermat's Last Theorem*, Simon Singh

Your UCAS application and the Personal Statement

You apply to Oxford and Cambridge in the same way that you would apply to any other university: through the University and Colleges Admissions Service (UCAS). The UCAS form is a long document that is completed online and sent to all five of your chosen universities by 15 October. (For more advice about completing the UCAS form, see Appendix 3). It asks you to include details of your school(s), exam grades, employment experience, your choices of university in order of preference and a Personal Statement: a 47-line written document that outlines the reasons for your choice of subject.

Because most young people who apply to Oxbridge will have excellent grades (usually AAAA at A level) as well as a glowing report from their teachers, the UCAS Personal Statement is very important. This piece of writing provides the admissions tutor with the first glimpse of your personality and intellect, and is the closest thing they have to meeting you until the interviews in December. This is also the first example of your written work that they will see. Your Personal Statement needs to stand out from the piles of similar documents strewn across the admissions tutor's desk. You need to come across as someone they – and their colleagues – would be happy to teach for many hours. The Personal Statement, therefore, plays a large part in their decision about whether or not to invite you to interview. When the admissions tutor reads your Personal Statement, there are some very specific qualities he/she will look for. These qualities are listed below.

- *Proof that you have made an appropriate subject choice*
- *An ability to survive in an intense and pressured atmosphere*
- *A depth of interest in the subject*
- *An ability to study independently.*

Admissions Tutor, Cambridge

What exactly do the admissions tutors mean by this?

- They want to see that you have thought long and hard about what you want to study and why; that you have investigated the subject fully, through extensive reading.
- Pressure is high at Oxbridge, and students who apply to either Cambridge or Oxford must be prepared for this. Admissions tutors need to be sure that you are someone who will flourish in the intense environment. Not everyone does. If you have survived the pressures of multiple A level courses and exams, this is already a good sign. If, in addition, you show that you have been able to juggle several extra-curricular activities as well as undertaking research towards your university subject, then admissions tutors will recognise that you are a resilient student with stamina.
- Depth of interest in your subject is essential, as discussed previously. If you show that you have made a serious effort to read around your subject this sends positive signals to the admissions tutor. Even better, if you show that, whilst reading, you found an area within your discipline that interests you particularly, and then you have followed this up further with more in-depth study, you will have shown that you can undertake university level research and are deeply committed to your subject.
- If you have read above and beyond what your teachers have given you in class, you are showing proof of independent study that will be essential when you go to university. This also shows a deeper commitment to your subject and good studentship.

A model Personal Statement

There are no hard and fast rules about how to structure your Personal Statement. Below, however, is an example of how a well-organised statement might be written with a synopsis, paragraph by paragraph. Below each synopsis is an example of a paragraph written by a candidate who did get an interview at Cambridge to read economics. Read the example carefully, but do not be tempted to copy it.

The **first paragraph** should be punchy and attention grabbing. It should explain, in as few sentences as possible, why you are so excited to study your chosen subject and why you think it is worth studying.

> Physics answers the question of why? Maths is a tool to solve quantitative issues. Politics is the study of the structure of law, government and policy. Economics, as I see it, is everything in between.

In **paragraph two** you could discuss your particular interests in relation to your university subject choice. This is your chance to write about specific ideas you have developed as a result of reading beyond your A level syllabus, any visits that have inspired you, or work experience that has opened your mind to new ideas. Paragraphs one and two should take up about two-thirds of the entire statement.

> I thoroughly enjoy and am extremely interested in economics. The distinct view on the world that economists have and the power to do good are the reasons why I am so enthused about the subject. I'm particularly drawn to development economics, but acknowledge the role that other spheres of economics such as econometrics, micro and macroeconomics play in the constitution of this field. This is why my current goal as a student of economics is to learn as much about the subject in general. To this end, I have read several works of prominent economists. Delving into mind-expanding texts such as 'Development as Freedom', 'Capitalism and Freedom', 'Globalisation and its Discontents' and Adam Smith's 'Wealth of Nations'. In addition to my individual exploration, I have attended courses at Harvard University and at Brown University for Economics and Global Development respectively.

The **third paragraph** can start to incorporate your personal experiences and how these have shaped your academic interests and choice of university subject.

> My passion for economics, especially development economics, comes as a result of my background and experiences. I have been fortunate enough to travel, experience different cultures, lifestyles

and perspectives. Seeing suffering and poverty, through community service has made me internalise these issues. Possessing a heritage that combines both economically developed and developing nations (as I have lived in both Costa Rica and Britain) has underlined this problem for me. Throughout my life, I have seen myself as a problem-solver and I believe this has been highlighted through Young Enterprise. Being Head of Production, I was in charge of overcoming difficulties such as rising costs. We did not win in the end, but it was a great learning experience and one that showed me the importance of thinking creatively.

The **fourth paragraph** can include a brief summary of your extra-curricular activities. Remember, the admissions tutor will have to live with you for three years if you get in to his/her college. You need to come across as a responsible, friendly person who will be an asset, rather than an embarrassment, to the college's reputation. Finish off with a closing sentence that reminds the reader why you want to study the subject you have chosen.

Aside from travelling and learning, I appreciate the arts and sports greatly. Acting is a passion of mine and started by attending Theatre Saturday School at the age of six. Since then I have been involved in different types of work, for instance, I was involved with a professional children's production which produced the play 'Annie' and I played the lead male role.

Economics, however, has developed into my newest and greatest interest as it seems to combine not only all my academic endeavours but also permeates my pursuits out of the classroom.

When you have finished writing your Personal Statement, get your parents, older siblings and teachers to check it. Make sure there are no spelling errors and ask the people who read it whether it sounds like it was written by you. It is, after all, you who will be going to meet the admissions tutors, and you who want to be accepted by Oxbridge. Do not be tempted to plagiarise. Both universities have a computer system to spot plagiarism, and will automatically reject you if you have done this. Make sure, also, that you are prepared to discuss every piece of information in your Personal Statement if you are called to interview. Admissions tutors will almost certainly pick up on any books you say you have read as a conversation starter; so read them all again.

Extra-curricular activities and work experience

It is a good idea to discuss extra-curricular activities and work experience that is relevant to your chosen degree. It is very important that you weave these experiences into a discussion about why you want to study your subject. All the information you include must form part of a life story that seems to lead directly to your chosen undergraduate degree at Oxbridge. Below is a very good example of paragraph two from one student's Personal Statement. Her name is Laura, and she was asked to interview at Cambridge for medicine.

I organised some work experience in the orthopaedic wing of Nottingham Hospital and at my local GP clinic. At Nottingham Hospital, I shadowed the doctors on their ward round, watched a number of knee replacements and observed fracture clinic which made me realise how such a simple procedure can dramatically increase the quality of life in older people. This is such a stark contrast with my experiences in Uganda where living to 70 is seen as something of a miracle. A further thing I learnt from my work experience is the importance of patient–doctor relationships, and this is one of the factors which really draws me to medicine. I saw this most particularly in my work experience with a GP where I saw him take on a central role of trust within the community. I have had much opportunity to develop my interpersonal skills. During Sixth Form I worked with underprivileged children at an after-school club in London. I have volunteered in a charity shop and this year I am volunteering one day a week at St Peter's Hospice in Green Town. I am able to easily relate to people and enjoy meeting, getting to know and trying to help different people. I used this skill when I was deputy head girl of my school, where I was involved in talking to students and helping them with any problems they might have. I keep up to date with the news, reading about medical developments in the 'BMJ' and the 'New Scientist'.

Not only is Laura's work experience specifically relevant to medicine, but she has woven her experiences into a narrative that explains very clearly why she wants to study this subject at university and why she would be good at it.

Following is one more Personal Statement in its entirety. The author, Imogen, applied to Oxford to read French and Italian. She was invited to interview.

In a world where increasing numbers of people speak English, it may seem superfluous for students to put their efforts into acquiring foreign languages. For me, however, language is not just a means by which we communicate, but the barrier of language often hides whole worlds of literature and culture which can remain inaccessible, even through translation. For this reason, language as a whole is a source of fascination for me, resulting in a desire to focus on Italian, which I studied at A level, and French, a language I very much enjoyed at GCSE and which I feel complements Italian well. I have therefore resolved to take a one year French A level course during my gap year, enabling me to study it at university.

I think literature portrays language at its best, as it is the means by which a language displays the full range of its versatility and the essence of the people who communicate through it. It often offers a window into the culture it describes, which I feel is especially well achieved by Natalia Ginzburg. After studying 'Le Voci della Sera' at A level, I read 'La Strada che Va in Citta' and 'E Stato Cosi', finding that her depiction of the various female characters strongly impresses upon the reader the difficulties faced by these women in the light of their religion and community. One sympathises easily with them as they struggle to find happiness, owing largely to Ginzburg's simple and often stark narrative. Similarly, I admire Primo Levi for the style in which he narrates, maintaining a dignified approach to the experiences he describes. In 'Se Non Ora, Quando?' his depiction of Italy is striking: an oasis of freedom, where Jews and Christians are indistinguishable.

To help improve my French I have read various works of literature and philosophy. I became interested in the problem of evil through my Philosophy A level, so I read Voltaire's 'Zadig', which demonstrates how suffering is unavoidable, but that sense and perseverance will see a man through. This, however, does little to solve the theological problem of evil. Nor does Candide 12 years later, but it highlights flaws in the ideology that 'tout est au mieux', or 'all is for the best', and points forward to suggest how to live happily in spite of evil. I sub-scribe to the literary magazine 'Virgule', through which I discovered Pierre de Ronsard, in whom I was delighted to find traces of Petrarch, by whom I have read some Canzoniere, and numerous classical authors that I have studied. I read a selection of Les Amours, and found that there was much opportunity for intertextual comparison with the texts I have studied in the past.

Last summer I worked as an au pair in France, which improved my French enormously, not only giving me an understanding of French daily life, but also valuable experience of the world of work. At school I was awarded the Prize for Classics and Italian, for linguistic success and contribution to these areas. Outside academic concerns, I was a Managing Director of a Young Enterprise company in Year 12, and have completed the Silver Duke of Edinburgh award, as well as a qualification in youth leadership, which I hope have made me responsible and motivated. In addition to playing the piano, I sang in two choirs at school and continue to take lessons, focusing on Italian arias. Alongside my studies this year, I follow Italian current affairs by transcribing the TG2 news, and am taking conversation classes weekly. I am also taking classes at the Institut Français in London to help me become more fluent in French, and shall continue to read avidly, exploring as many authors as possible.

Additional form for Cambridge: the Supplementary Application Questionnaire (SAQ)

Once you have completed your Personal Statement and sent off your UCAS form, the Cambridge Admissions Office will automatically email you an additional questionnaire to complete: the SAQ. The SAQ is filled out online, costs nothing to send, and gives Cambridge more information about you and your application. If you do not have access to email you can contact the Cambridge Admissions Office for a paper version.

The initial email will give you all the information you need in order to complete the form correctly, as well as a deadline (usually the end of October).

The SAQ includes the following eight sections.

1| **Photograph.** You will need a passport-sized colour photograph of yourself, preferably in digital format, which can then be uploaded onto the form.
2| **Application type.** This section asks questions about your application, such as whether you have applied for an organ scholarship, if you are taking a gap year or whether you are going through the Special Access Scheme.
3| **Personal details.** This covers information about you and your own situation, such as where you live, what your first name is, etc.
4| **Course details.** Here you need to declare your preferred course options (if applicable); for example, if you are applying to read modern and medieval languages, you state which languages you wish to study in this section.
5| **Education.** In this section, you will need to give information about your school(s), such as class sizes and descriptions of any extra help you may have received towards your application.
6| **Qualifications.** In this section, you need to give details of your AS and/or A level modules, or their equivalents, and your marks.
7| **Additional information.** This is where you can add an additional Personal Statement. You will also need to discuss your career plans and give some proof of your interest in your chosen subject (for example details of your work experience).
8| **Submit.**

The Additional Personal Statement is the perfect opportunity for you to explain to the admissions tutor how excited you are about the course and perhaps the college to which you are applying. Do take advantage of this extra space to make an impression. Remember, however, not to duplicate anything you have said on the UCAS form.

While your UCAS Personal Statement will be seen by every institution you apply to, the SAQ is for the admissions tutors at Cambridge only. This means that you can discuss particular elements of the course content or programme at Cambridge without putting any other university off. Make the most of this and explain why their course and teaching staff are perfect for you, and why you will fit in particularly well there. Remember also that by mentioning your areas of special academic interest, you will encourage predictable question at interview, making it easier to prepare thoroughly.

Here is a good example written by a student for his economics application.

I am particularly interested in studying economics at Cambridge as the faculty stresses its commitment to public policy, and I share the view of its importance to the functioning of our daily lives. The course is particularly suited to my interests as I would have the opportunity to specialise in development economics and I would enjoy the academic rigour of applying maths to the analysis of economics. Furthermore, I would be able to draw from my other interests such as politics and history to augment my study of economics. I have started to use SPSS software in order to enhance my theoretical understanding of econometrics and because I enjoy using quantitative methods.

I find the collegiate nature of the university attractive because I love talking about the subject, and nothing is as enjoyable as to share one's interest with others who feel the same way about it! Also, as someone who values perspective, I think that discussing issues with people from different disciplines would facilitate the exchange of ideas and present new angles from which to address points of interest. I am also excited at the opportunity to discuss ideas in supervisions with people who are at the forefront of their field and who are engaged in active research.

Here's another example written by a modern languages applicant.

I am looking forward with confidence and enthusiasm to the challenge of completing French A level in the coming year before embarking on a modern languages degree course. Cambridge's emphasis on literature mirrors my own enthusiasm for French and Italian literature, and I was particularly thrilled to note that several lecturers have expertise in the works of Primo Levi, for whom I have great admiration, and who I would love to study at a higher level. As I am thinking

> of becoming a teacher, the idea of the year abroad greatly appeals, as it would give me valuable experience of teaching whilst improving my linguistic fluency.

Oxford no longer requires an additional form, with the three exceptions of: candidates for choral or organ awards, candidates wishing to be interviewed overseas and graduate applicants for the Accelerated Medical Course. Some of the information which the Cambridge SAQ requires is collected in Oxford's case from the government's public information service. The information that the university will look at is as follows:

- the performance of your school or college at GCSE and A level or their equivalents, both using DCSF or equivalent data (in both instances a candidate will be flagged if their educational establishment performs below the national average)
- the postcode of your home, assessed using Acorn information (where a candidate's postcode falls into groups four or five the application will be flagged)
- whether you have been looked after/in care for more than three months (determined from the UCAS application)
- whether you have participated in either a Sutton Trust summer school or the Oxford Young Ambassador Scheme.

Submitting written work

Another way admissions tutors decide whether or not to interview you – if you are applying for an essay-based subject – is by looking at a sample of your written work. This is something that you need to consider once you have submitted your application form(s). By looking at one of your essays, the admissions tutors will be able to assess your ability to research, organise information, form opinions and construct a coherent and cogent argument in writing. These are essential skills to have when studying an essay subject at Oxbridge, and the admissions tutors need to see that you have these skills, and the potential to improve.

Normally the essay that you send will have been written as part of your A level course. Make sure that you send a particularly good example of your work; ask your teachers to suggest changes and then to remark the essay when you have improved it as much as possible. Do not, however, submit anything that could not have been written by you. Plagiarism will be very obvious to admissions tutors and could potentially get you into some tricky situations at interview since submitted written work is often discussed at interview.

The submitted essay is often used as the starting point for discussion in the interview. The essay can show us whether the candidate has the ability to argue and has academic confidence.

Admissions Tutor, Cambridge

The Oxford prospectus gives clear instructions about what you need to send and when. Remember to inform your teachers in advance that you will need to send marked work.

At Cambridge each college has a different policy on written work, but you are more likely to be asked to send in work if you are applying to read an arts or social sciences subject. The college will contact you directly if they require work from you.

If you have applied to Oxford, you will need to submit marked work for the following subjects:

- archaeology and anthropology
- classical archaeology and ancient history
- classics
- classics and English
- classics and modern languages
- classics and oriental studies
- computer science
- economics and management
- English and modern languages
- English language and literature
- European and Middle Eastern languages
- experimental psychology
- fine art
- geography
- history
- history (ancient and modern)
- history and economics
- history and English
- history and modern languages
- history and politics
- history of art
- law (jurisprudence) and law with law studies in Europe
- mathematics
- mathematics and computer science
- mathematics and philosophy
- mathematics and statistics
- medicine
- modern languages
- modern languages and linguistics
- music
- oriental studies

- philosophy and modern languages
- philosophy and theology
- physics
- physics and philosophy
- physiological sciences
- PPE
- PPP
- theology.

04 Written tests

As more and more students are achieving As at A level, both Oxford and Cambridge are increasingly relying on other testing systems when selecting candidates for interview. These tests include the BMAT for medicine and the LNAT for law at Oxford: two externally administered tests. The HAT is sat for history at Oxford and there are various similar but internal exams set by Cambridge colleges. STEP papers have been reintroduced for maths at Cambridge as well as the TSA (Thinking Skills Assessment) for various other Cambridge subjects. Not only do these exams aim to highlight the best students when A levels seem to be failing, they also aim to widen access. Since it is often difficult to revise for the Oxbridge written tests, students have to rely on their innate intellectual creativity to complete them. In this way poorly schooled children are at no disadvantage.

The style of testing also differs from what many school leavers will be used to. Whereas A levels often test factual recall, the Oxbridge written exams look for analytical and critical capabilities. It should be noted, therefore, that these tests are likely to be much harder than anything you will have experienced at school. This is taken into consideration, and admissions tutors do not expect students to achieve 100%.

Oxford and Cambridge take quite different approaches to additional written tests. Oxford exams are standardised: for example, all students applying for history across the whole university will take exactly the same test (the HAT). In comparison, Cambridge tests vary from college to college: history applicants to Trinity, Girton and Claire College might be set three completely different questions.

Testing happens at various stages during the application process. Some tests are sat in early November at your school (the BMAT, LNAT and ELAT, for example). The results of these tests can then play a large part in determining whether you are called to interview in the first place. Some tests – including the majority of those for Cambridge – take place when you go up for interview in early December. The results are then used, alongside your interview performance, to decide whether you should be made a conditional offer.

The following chapter aims to give an account of the various written test students face prior to/during their interviews including: the deadlines for registering for the exams; when and where the tests are sat; details about the structure of the tests, including knowledge requirements; sample questions; and useful links for more information and practice.

Tables 3 and 4 explain which subjects require additional written tests at Oxford and Cambridge respectively. However, it is a good idea to check this information by ringing the admissions tutor at your college directly (see the college or university prospectus for the telephone number) or by going to the web addresses below.

- **Cambridge:** www.cam.ac.uk/admissions/undergraduate/courses
- **Oxford:** www.admissions.ox.ac.uk/interviews/tests

Table 3: Subjects tested at Oxford before the interview

Subject	Test
Economics and management	TSA (Thinking Skills Assessment)
English	ELAT (English Literature Aptitude Test)
Experimental psychology	TSA (specialist version)
History	HAT (History Aptitude Test)
Law	LNAT (The National Admissions Test for Law)
Maths (and all joint degrees including maths)	Aptitude test for maths and computer science
Medicine and physiological sciences	BMAT (BioMedical Aptitude Test)
Physics (and all joint degrees including physics)	Physics Aptitude Test
PPE	TSA (specialist version)
PPP	TSA (specialist version)

Table 4: Subjects tested at Cambridge before the interview

Subject	Test
Computer science, economics, engineering, land economy, natural sciences and SPS	TSA (used by some colleges)
Maths	STEP (Sixth Term Examination Papers)(used by almost all colleges)
Medicine and veterinary medicine	BMAT(BioMedical Admissions Test)

■ BMAT (BioMedical Admissions Test), Oxford and Cambridge

For applications to medicine, physiological sciences (Oxford) and veterinary science (Cambridge):

- Register online by the last week in September with a fee of £32.10 (waiveable).

- Sit the BMAT in the first week of November at your school.
- Go to www.bmat.org.uk/faqstudent.html#gen15 for more information.

Both Oxford and Cambridge require students applying for medical school and for veterinary science to sit the BMAT exam. It aims to predict your potential as a medical student.

Structure: it is a two-hour paper that is sat at your school and there are three sections:

1| aptitude and skills (60 minutes, multiple choice)
2| scientific knowledge and applications (30 minutes, multiple choice)
3| essay writing task (30 minutes).

The BMAT requires GCSE-level knowledge of maths and GCSE Dual Science Award knowledge of biology, chemistry and physics. The exam is structured so that biology, chemistry and physics are equally weighted and maths is slightly less important.

Oxford and Cambridge will look at the scores of each section individually. Cambridge admissions tutors believe that Sections 1 and 2 correlate best with Tripos performance and therefore put an emphasis on these sections.

Perhaps the most important thing to prepare for with the BMAT is timing. There is relatively little time to get through a vast number of questions. You need to know the relevant A level and GCSE courses like the back of your hand so that you can apply your knowledge to complex situations without having to stop and think.

BMAT example questions

Section 1 question 2

'The UK government wishes to increase the number of young people from poorer families entering university education. However, it has recently changed the way in which it provides financial support for students. Whereas it used to provide grants that the student did not need to repay, it now provides loans that the student must repay when he or she enters employment. Research shows that students from poorer families are more likely to be deterred from going to university by the prospect of debt.'

Which one of the following is an inference that can be drawn from the passage above?

A   Students from poorer families are less interested in entering university.
B   Universities will not be willing to help meet the government's target.
C   The government's action is likely to deter poorer students from going to university more than richer.

D   The prospect of debt is a deterrent to all students, not just the poorer ones.

E   Maintenance grants were too expensive for the government to fund.

Section 3 — writing task (30 minutes)

Our genes evolved for a Stone Age life style. Therefore, we must adopt Stone Age habits if we are to be healthy.

Write a unified essay in which you address the following.

- Explain the logical connection between the two sentences.
- What might be the practical implications if we were to agree with the reasoning?
- Discuss the extent to which the argument is valid.

Source: From the specimen papers available on the Cambridge Assessment website (www.admissionstests.cambridgeassessment.org.uk) Reprinted by permission of the University of Cambridge Local Examinations Syndicate.

■ ELAT (English Literature Aptitude Test), Oxford only

- Register online by mid-October.
- Sit ELAT in the first week of November at your school.
- Go to www.elat.org.uk for more information.

The ELAT tests the ability to read unfamiliar texts closely and to construct a focused essay.

Structure: the ELAT lasts for 90 minutes. You will be given six poems or prose passages and will be asked compare and contrast two or three of them. All six passages will be linked in some way and this will be made clear in the question. Your score will be placed into one of four bands, and those whose scores lie in the top two bands are the most likely to be called for interview.

ELAT sample questions

The following poems and extracts from longer texts present views of fathers, mainly as seen by their children. Read all the material carefully, and then complete the task below.

(a) An extract from a novel by Philip Roth, *The Human Stain*, published in 2001.

(b) 'To the Reverend Shade of His Religious Father', a poem by Robert Herrick (1591–1674).

(c) An extract from a novel by Samuel Richardson, *Clarissa*, 1740, vol. 1, Letter VIII. The novel is written entirely as a sequence of letters.

(d) 'Carousel', a poem by Lucinda Roy; first published in 1988.

(e) 'Father's Bedroom', a poem by Robert Lowell (1917–1977).

(f) An extract from a short story, 'Grocer's Daughter', published in 1987, by Marianne Wiggins.

Task

Select two or three of the passages (a) to (f) and compare and contrast them in any ways that seem interesting to you, paying particular attention to distinctive features of structure, language and style. In your introduction, indicate briefly what you intend to explore or illustrate through close reading of your chosen passages.

This task is designed to assess your responsiveness to unfamiliar literary material and your skills in close reading. Marks are not awarded for references to other texts or authors you have studied.

Source: From the specimen papers available on the Cambridge Assessment website (www.admissionstests.cambridgeassessment.org.uk). Reprinted by permission of the University of Cambridge Local Examinations Syndicate.

■ HAT (History Aptitude Test), Oxford only

■   Register online by mid-October.

■   Sit the HAT in the first week of November at your school.

■   Go to www.history.ox.ac.uk/prosundergrad/applying/hat_introduction for more information.

The HAT will require you to discuss one of the historical periods you have studied at A level, so revision is essential. Oxford will automatically send the HAT results to your school. In general, the people who score in the bottom 20% of HAT will be deselected.

The HAT tests the following skills and attributes:

■   the ability to read carefully and critically

■   the adoption of an analytical approach

■   the ability to answer a question relevantly

■   the ability to offer a coherent argument

■   precision in the handling of concepts and in the selection of evidence presented to support points

■   historical imagination

■   originality

■   precision, clarity and facility of writing.

Make sure, when writing about a subject that you know well, to keep tightly to your plan, and not to get carried away displaying your knowledge. For the HAT, structure is incredibly important.

Structure of the test

The HAT website states:

> *The HAT lasts for two hours and has two elements: a series of questions, including a short essay, based on a short piece of historical writing; and a single question, based on a primary source. Candidates are advised to spend about 40 minutes on reading the texts, thinking about them and planning their answers. The rest of the time they should spend on writing. Guidance is given about the form and length of each answer.*

www.history.ox.ac.uk/prosundergrad/applying/hat_introduction

Section One (75–80 minutes, including reading, thinking and planning time). This section comprises three questions and is worth 70/100 marks:

1| Definition exercise. Understanding and defining terms drawn from the text. Relates to: careful and critical reading; precision in the handling of concepts; precision, clarity and facility of writing. (10/100 marks)
2| Explanation exercise. Analysing and explaining terms drawn from the text. Relates to: careful and critical reading; analytical approach; precision in the handling of concepts; precision, clarity and facility of writing. (20/100 marks)
3| Essay exercise. Applying a concept/hypothesis from the text to a historical situation; writing cogently at length. Relates to: analytical approach; coherent argument; precision in the handling of concepts and selection of evidence; relevance to the question; historical imagination; originality; precision, clarity and facility of writing. (40/100 marks)

Section Two (40–45 minutes, including reading, thinking and planning time). This section comprises one question and is worth 30/100 marks:

1| Interpretation exercise. Interpretative response to primary source. Relates to: careful and critical reading; historical imagination; originality; precision, clarity and facility of writing.

Information taken from the Oxford undergraduate prospectus online: www.history.ox.ac.uk/prosundergrad/applying/hat_introduction

---

HAT example question

Oxford Colleges History Aptitude Test. October 31st 2007. For the full exam and its accompanying mark scheme go to: www.history. ox.ac.uk/prosundergrad/applying/hat_introduction.

Question 2 (30 marks)

The following extract from *The History of the Franks* was written by Gregory, Bishop of Tours, and completed in AD594. The events he

---

describes occurred about 90 years before he wrote. Tours was in the territory ruled by the successors of Clovis.

You are not expected to know anything about Clovis or the period. You must read carefully and critically, and use your skills of historical analysis to interpret the extract.

> While Clovis1 was in Paris, he sent secretly to Chloderic, the son of Sigibert2, saying 'Your father is old. If he were to die, his kingdom would come to you of right and my alliance would come with it.' Chloderic was led astray by his lust for power and began to plot his father's death. He set assassins on him and had him murdered, so that he might gain possession of his kingdom. By the judgement of God, Chloderic fell into the same pit that he had dug for his father. He sent messengers to King Clovis to announce his father's death. 'My father is dead,' said he, 'and I have taken over his kingdom and his treasure. Send me your envoys and I will gladly hand over to you anything that you may care to select from this treasure.' 'I thank you for your good will,' answered Clovis. 'I ask you to show all your treasure to my messengers, but you may keep it . . .' [The envoys came, saw the treasure and encouraged Chloderic to finger the gold in a chest] As he leaned forward to do this, one of the Franks raised his double-headed axe and split Chloderic's skull. This unworthy son thus shared the fate of his father. When Clovis heard that both were dead, he came to Cologne himself and ordered the inhabitants to assemble. 'Chloderic, the son of your King, my brother, was plotting against his father and putting it out that I wanted him killed. As Sigibert fled, Chloderic had him murdered. While Chloderic was showing his father's treasure, he in turn was killed by somebody or other. I take no responsibility for what has happened. It is not for me to shed the blood of one of my fellow kings, for that is a crime. But since things have turned out this way, you should turn to me and put yourselves under my protection.' The men of Cologne clashed their shields and shouted their approval; they raised Clovis on a shield and made him their ruler. Thus he took over both the kingship and the treasure and submitted Sigibert's people to his own rule. Day in day out God submitted the enemies of Clovis to his dominion and increased his power, for he walked before him with an upright heart and did what was pleasing in his sight.

What does this extract tell us about kingship among the Franks in the 6th century? (Write about one to two sides.)

Source: This question is taken from the HAT paper for 2008 (www.history.ox.ac.uk/ prosundergrad/applying/documents/HAT_paper_2008.pdf). This and all other HAT papers can be accessed at: www.history.ox.ac.uk/prosundergrad/applying/ hat_introduction.htm.

■ LNAT (Law National Admissions Test), Oxford only

- Register online by mid-October and pay £40 (waiveable)
- Sit the test from early September and before the 1 November at a special test centre
- Go to www.lnat.ac.uk for more information.

The first part of the LNAT – a multiple-choice section – is machine-marked and the results are passed in numerical form to universities that participate in the LNAT selection process. You will only receive your marks after the admissions process is over. The second part of the LNAT, an essay section, is passed unmarked to LNAT-participating universities.

Structure: the LNAT is a two-hour test and has two parts: a multiple-choice element (80 minutes) and an essay element (40 minutes).

> The multiple-choice element consists of 10 argumentative passages, with three multiple-choice questions on each, making 30 questions in all. The questions are designed to test powers of comprehension, interpretation, analysis, synthesis, induction and deduction. These are the verbal reasoning skills at the heart of legal education. The questions do not test (and do not require) knowledge of any subject except for the English language.

> The essay element gives you a choice of questions on a range of subjects. Although these typically require some rudimentary knowledge of everyday subjects, the point is not to test that knowledge but your ability to argue economically to a conclusion with a good command of written English. This part of the test is not centrally assessed.

Information taken from the LNAT website: www.lnat.ac.uk/2009/introduction/test.html

For practice questions and mark schemes go to the LNAT website: www.lnat.ac.uk.

■ Aptitude test for maths and computer science, Oxford only

For applications to maths, maths with computer science, philosophy, statistics, or computer sciences.

- Sit the test at your school at the end of October or beginning of November.
- Your school will be sent the papers automatically.
- Go to www.maths.ox.ac.uk/prospective-students/undergraduate/specimen-tests to see the syllabus for the exam and specimen papers.

Testing for maths and sciences at Oxford (and Cambridge) is largely based upon AS level knowledge. It is often the case, however, that relatively simple facts and formulas must be remembered in order to apply them to more complex and novel contexts. In this way, students must be able think 'outside the box' creatively. The test is set with the aim of being approachable by all students, including those without a Further Mathematics A level, and those from other educational systems (e.g. Baccalaureate and Scottish Highers). It aims to test the depth of mathematical understanding of a student in the fourth term of their A levels (or equivalent) rather than a breadth of knowledge.

It is crucial that you do well in this paper since Oxford offers interviews based on student's success in the Aptitude Test:

> *Applicants will be shortlisted on the basis of the test score, together with information from applicants' UCAS forms and those shortlisted, in the UK and Europe, will be invited to Oxford in mid-December for interview. The expected proportion of applicants shortlisted is currently under review.*

www.maths.ox.ac.uk/prospective-students/undergraduate/ specimen-tests

Structure: the test lasts two and a half hours and there are seven questions in total. The first question is multiple choice and contains 10 parts each worth four marks. Marks are given solely for the correct answers, although applicants are encouraged to show any working in the space provided. Questions 2–7 are longer questions, each worth 15 marks, and candidates will need to show their working. Candidates should attempt four questions from 2–7, the selection depending on the degree for which they are applying. Details of precisely which questions you should attempt are given in the rubric on the front page of the test and throughout the paper.

■ *No calculators, formula sheets or dictionaries are permitted during the test.*
■ *Only answers written in the booklet will be marked. There are spare blank pages at the end of the test paper.*
■ *Further credit cannot be gained by attempting questions other than those appropriate to the degree applied for.*

Information taken from Oxford Mathematics faculty website: www.maths.ox.ac.uk/ prospective-students/undergraduate/specimen-tests

You should attempt some of the specimen/past tests provided on the website provided, so that you develop a sense of the format and style of the test, but no further preparation or practice, beyond work for A levels, is needed. Whilst two of the tests provided on the site are specimens, almost all the questions included were set on previous years' entrance tests.

Physics and maths test for physics, Oxford only

For applications to physics or physics and philosophy.

- Test papers are automatically sent to your school.
- Sit the test in the first week of November at your school.
- Go to www.physics.ox.ac.uk/contact/ for more information on the physics department at Oxford.

There are two separate syllabi: one for physics and another for maths for physics (A and B). Following is an outline of both. Oxford makes clear that the great majority of the knowledge required for this test will be familiar from GCSE and AS level mathematics and physics and that shortlisting for interview is largely based on the results of this aptitude test.

Syllabus for Part A of the aptitude test (mathematics for physics)

- **Elementary mathematics:** knowledge of elementary mathematics, in particular topics in arithmetic, geometry including coordinate geometry, and probability, will be assumed.
- **Algebra:** properties of polynomials, including the solution of quadratics; graph sketching and transformations of variables; inequalities and their solution; elementary trigonometry including relationships between sin, cos and tan (sum and difference formulae will be stated if required); properties of logarithms and exponentials; arithmetic and geometric progressions and the binomial expansion.
- **Calculus:** differentiation and integration of polynomials including fractional and negative powers (but not integration of $1/x$); differentiation as finding the slope of a curve, and the location of maxima, minima and points of inflection; integration as the reverse of differentiation and as finding the area under a curve; simplifying integrals by symmetry arguments.
- **Physics:** knowledge of elementary physics will be assumed; questions may require the manipulation of mathematical expressions in a physical context.

Candidates who have studied mathematics at GCSE and AS level (including the first two core pure modules) should be familiar with the great majority of the syllabus.

Syllabus for Part B of the aptitude test (physics)

- **Mechanics:** distance, velocity, speed, acceleration, and the relationships between them; interpretation of graphs; response to forces (Newton's laws of motion; weight and mass; addition of forces; circular motion); friction, air resistance, and terminal velocity; levers, pulleys and other elementary machines; springs and Hooke's law; kinetic and potential energy and their inter-conversion; other forms of energy; conservation of energy; power and work.

- **Waves and optics:** longitudinal and transverse waves; amplitude, frequency, period, wavelength and speed, and the relationships between them; basic properties of the electromagnetic spectrum; reflection at plane mirrors; refraction and elementary properties of prisms and lenses including total internal reflection (mathematical treatment not required); elementary understanding of interference and diffraction (mathematical treatment not required).
- **Electricity and magnetism:** current, voltage (potential difference), charge, resistance; relationships between them and links to energy and power; elementary circuits including batteries, wires, resistors, filament lamps, diodes, capacitors, light dependent resistors and thermistors; series and parallel circuits; elementary electrostatic forces and magnetism (mathematical treatment not required); links between electricity and magnetism; electromagnets, motors, generators and transformers; current as a flow of electrons; thermionic emission and energy of accelerated electron beams.
- **The natural world:** atomic and nuclear structure; properties of alpha, beta and gamma radiation; half lives; nuclear fission; structure of the solar system; phases of the moon and eclipses; elementary treatment of circular orbits under gravity including orbital speed, radius, period, centripetal acceleration, and gravitational centripetal force; satellites; geostationary and polar orbits elementary properties of solids, liquids and gases including responses to pressure and temperature.
- **Mathematics:** knowledge of elementary mathematics will be assumed; questions may require the manipulation of mathematical expressions in a physical context.
- **Problem-solving:** problems may be set which require problem solving based on information provided rather than knowledge about a topic.

Candidates who have studied physics at Higher Tier GCSE or AS level should be familiar with the great majority of the syllabus (www.physics. ox.ac.uk/admissions/syllabus.htm).

◼ TSA (Thinking Skills Assessment), Oxford and Cambridge

For applicants to Cambridge to read: computer science, economics, engineering, natural sciences, land economy, philosophy and PPS. For applications to Oxford to read: economics and management, PPE, experimental psychology and computer science.

- Register by mid-October online.
- Sit the test at your school in the first week of November.

■ Go to www.admissionstests.cambridgeassessment.org.uk for more information and specimen papers.

This test aims to measure your critical thinking and problem solving skills, and is used to decide whether you should be asked to interview.

Structure: the TSA is a 90-minute multiple choice test consisting of 50 questions. There are two types of question in the test:

1| The **problem-solving** category is concerned with numerical and spatial reasoning (both understanding arguments and reasoning using everyday language). You may be asked to sift through information to identify important points or to compare or match argument structures.

2| The **critical-thinking** questions can involve the following:

■ summarising the main point
■ identifying an assumption
■ drawing a conclusion
■ identifying flaws in an argument
■ understanding the structure of an argument
■ applying principles.

Each question is worth one mark.

TSA example questions

Cambridge – Specimen paper section 1 question 3

Every year in Britain there are nearly 25,000 car fires, yet it is estimated that only 5% of motorists travel with a fire extinguisher in their car. If more motorists could be encouraged to carry fire extinguishers then the number of car fires could be considerably reduced.

Which of the following is the best statement of the flaw in the argument above?

A It ignores the fact that millions of motorists never experience a car fire.

B It assumes that carrying a fire extinguisher will enable fires to be put out.

C It implies that the occurrence of car fires is related to the lack of an extinguisher.

D It overlooks the possibility that fires might not be put out with an extinguisher.

E It ignores the fact that there are different extinguishers for different kinds of fires.

Source: From the specimen papers available on the Cambridge Assessment website (www.admissionstests.cambridgeassessment.org.uk) by permission of the University of Cambridge Local Examinations Syndicate

---

◼ STEP (Sixth Term Examination Papers), Cambridge only

For applications to study mathematics and mathematics with physics, engineering and computer science.

- The exam is taken in June at your school at the same time as your A levels.
- Your school must contact the Admissions Testing office at Cambridge (01223 558455) to request the STEP papers.
- Go to www.maths.cam.ac.uk/undergrad/admissions/step for more information.

Cambridge normally asks for STEPs as part of a conditional offer for maths and sometimes for the other subjects mentioned above. Whereas A level exam papers cannot be seen by universities, Cambridge admissions tutors can look at your STEP answer papers, thereby identifying your strengths and weaknesses more accurately. It is also important to realise that these exams are harder than A levels, and to adjust your expectations accordingly:

STEP is supposed to be difficult: it is aimed at the top 5% or so of all A level mathematics candidates. It is therefore important to adjust your sights when tackling a STEP paper. The questions are much longer and more demanding than A level questions (they are intended to take about 45 minutes, rather than the 10 or so minutes for an A level question). They therefore look daunting; but you should not be daunted. In recent years, you only had to give good (not perfect) answers to four questions for a grade 1.

**Information taken from the Cambridge website:
www.maths.cam.ac.uk/undergrad/admissions/step**

Structure: there are three STEP mathematics papers, numbered I, II and III. Your offer will usually include grades in two of the papers, normally I and II if you are not taking the full Further Mathematics A level (or an equivalent qualification) or II and III if you are taking Further Mathematics A level (or an equivalent qualification).

Each paper consists of 13 questions: eight pure, three mechanics, and two statistics and probability. Each paper is assessed on answers to at most six questions. There are five grades, which are (from highest to lowest) S, 1, 2, 3, and U.

> *The syllabus for Mathematics I and II is based on a typical single subject A level syllabus: the Pure Mathematics content is very slightly more than the A level common core. The syllabuses for the Mechanics and the Probability and Statistics sections are each equivalent to two or three A level modules but, since there is no common core for these areas, the material may not coincide with the modules of your particular A level. Paper I is intended specifically for candidates who are not taking Further Mathematics (or the equivalent) and the questions are intended to be easier than those in Paper II. The syllabus for Mathematics III is based on a typical Further Mathematics A level syllabus (there is no Further Mathematics core syllabus) and the questions are intended to be of about the same level of difficulty as those of Paper II.*

Information taken from the Cambridge website:
www.maths.cam.ac.uk/undergrad/admissions/step

The best way to prepare is to work through past exam papers. The following example will give you an idea of the sorts of questions you may be asked.

STEP 2008 Paper ii Section C: Probability and Statistics

Question 12

In the High Court of Farnia, the outcome of each case is determined by three judges: the ass, the beaver and the centaur. Each judge decides its verdict independently. Being simple creatures, they make their decisions entirely at random. Past verdicts show that the ass gives a guilty verdict with probability p, the beaver gives a guilty verdict with probability $p/3$ and the centaur gives a guilty verdict with probability $p2$.

Let X be the number of guilty verdicts given by the three judges in a case. Given that $E(X) = 4/3$, find the value of p. The probability that a defendant brought to trial is guilty is t. The King pronounces that the defendant is guilty if at least two of the judges give a guilty verdict; otherwise, he pronounces the defendant not guilty. Find the value of t such that the probability that the King pronounces correctly is $1/2$.

Source: From the specimen papers available on the Cambridge Assessment
website (www.admissionstests.cambridgeassessment.org.uk) by permission
of the University of Cambridge Local Examinations Syndicate

Useful links and resources for mathematics test preparation

- **STEP Specification:** this can be found on the CA website (www.stepmathematics.org.uk) and at the end of the Advanced Problems in the Core Mathematics booklet.
- **Advanced Problems in Core Mathematics:** (www.maths.cam.ac.uk/undergrad/admissions/step/advpcm.pdf): a booklet by Stephen Siklos, containing general advice on problem solving accompanied by 70 or so problems with hints and full solutions, and the STEP syllabuses. This would be a good starting point for your preparation.
- **AskNRICH:** (www.nrich.maths.org/askedNRICH/edited/menu/step.html) collated answers to STEP-related questions fielded by the AskNRICH project.
- **Miekleriggs Mathematics:** (www.meikleriggs.org.uk) Dr Peter Mitchell's website contains lots of useful mathematics including complete solutions to STEP papers from past years.
- **Stephen Siklos's website:** (www.damtp.cam.ac.uk/user/stcs) this contains some additional material, including a few video solutions of STEP questions.
- **Advanced Problems in Mathematics:** this booklet by Stephen Siklos consists of 43 STEP-like problems with discussion, hints and full solutions. It is available, at modest price, from OCR publications. But beware: it was written before the current syllabuses were in place.

For more information or help booking your test you can also email the Cambridge Assessment help line: stepinfo@cambridgeassessment.org.uk; or ring the help desk: 01223 558455.

■ Tests for modern languages, Oxford and Cambridge

- Normally taken when you go up for interview.
- Specimens for tests at Oxford: www.ox.ac.uk/admissions/undergraduate_ courses/how_to_apply/tests/specimens_of_written.html
- Specimens for Cambridge tests: www.mml.cam.ac.uk/prospectus/undergrad/applying/test.html

The modern languages courses at Oxford and Cambridge place emphasis on different aspects of language. The Cambridge course focuses on literature and culture, Oxford on grammar and linguistics. The tests taken just before interview at the universities reflect these differences. You will not be expected to have practised this type of test before, and will be at no disadvantage if you have not. The Cambridge admissions website is keen to reassure you:

> The test forms just one small part of the overall assessment of applicants (based on your written application, your school/college

record, interviews, etc.): even if you do not do particularly well at this written test, it is perfectly possible for you still to be offered a place.

www.mml.cam.ac.uk/prospectus/undergrad/applying/test.html

The structure is as follows.

■ The **Oxford** test is usually a 30-minute-long test and is divided into two sections. The first asks you to analyse the grammar of short sentences in your chosen language. The second section is a short translation from the target language that you wish to study at university back into English.

■ At **Cambridge**, you will be given 45 minutes to read a brief passage in English (300–350 words) and then asked to answer two or three questions about it.

You will write your answer in the target language that you are studying at A level (A2) or equivalent and for which you are applying to study at Cambridge University. The questions will contain an element of comprehension but will also invite you to add ideas of your own. In other words, the exercise is a combination of comprehension and free composition. The purpose is to see how you write in the foreign language: i.e. it assesses you grammar, accuracy, ability to express ideas, and vocabulary, though you are not expected to know the exact foreign-language term for each English term in the passage.

www.mml.cam.ac.uk/prospectus/undergrad/applying/test.html

Specimen for Cambridge comprehension test

You have **45 minutes** to complete this exercise.

Please read carefully the following passage and then write a single short essay which answers all the questions below. Please make your essay a total of 200–250 words long, no more and no less. Please answer in ONE of the modern languages that you are applying to study here, i.e. in a language that you are studying or have studied at A level (A2) or equivalent. If you are studying at A level (A2) or equivalent both of the languages that you wish to study here, then you're free to choose which of those two languages to write in.

The purpose of the exercise is for us to see how you write in the foreign language, to assess your grammar, your accuracy, your ability to express ideas, and your vocabulary, though we don't expect you to know the exact foreign-language term for each English term in the passage.

---

05 The interview

The interview is the single most important part of the selection process at Oxford and Cambridge and it happens in the first few weeks of December. This is the first time that your potential tutors or supervisors will meet you. You may look great on paper – have a brilliant Personal Statement and faultless exam grades – but you must make a good impression at interview too in order to be selected. Oxford and Cambridge interview about 90% of the students who apply. This means that, if everything else has gone to plan so far, it is likely you will get the chance to impress the tutors at your chosen college in person. However so will everyone else. The competition is still very high!

If you do get asked for interview, you will be sent a letter and email any time between mid-November and early December. This letter will give you the dates and times when you are required, and directions for how to get there. On arriving at Oxford or Cambridge you will normally go straight to your college: this is where you will be based for the duration of your stay. At this point you will get your interview timetable, a map of the university grounds and of the college.

If you need to stay overnight, you will be given a room of your own and free food will be available at set times of day in college 'halls' (the canteen). Accommodation will be free, and normally has en-suite bath and shower facilities. There are often current undergraduates on hand to usher interviewees to the right place at the right time, so you can be sure that you will be made comfortable and welcome. Remember, the porters – stationed near the front entrance in the 'porters' lodge' – love to be helpful; it's their job. If you have any questions about practical matters, or if you get lost, just head in their direction.

There are, however, a number of key differences between Oxford and Cambridge in terms of their interview practice.

- Cambridge interviews normally span one day only, Oxford between two and five.
- At Oxford it is possible to have interviews at other colleges during your stay, but first round interviews at Cambridge will take place at your college of choice only.
- Cambridge will tell you your interview date well in advance, Oxford will give you short notice and expect you to know when to arrive by the 'provisional date' section in the prospectus. Oxford reserves the right to call a candidate to interview any time up until a week before the provisional date given.

- Cambridge makes known individual interview start times and locations in advance, Oxford does not.
- Oxford will inform you of their decision before Christmas, Cambridge after.

Interview structure and layout

There are no hard and fast rules about how interviews at Oxford and Cambridge are structured, or how many interviewers there will be in the room with you at one time. There may just be one interviewer; there may be a panel of two or more. Each interview normally lasts 30–45 minutes and takes place in a room – normally the office of your potential tutor or director of studies – in the college. At Cambridge, candidates are often asked to attend two interviews over the period of one or two days: one is normally subject-specific, and the other is more general. Make sure you know which one you are walking into so that you can tailor your responses appropriately. It is not always obvious, so ask if you are uncertain. At Oxford, students are normally asked to stay over a period of several days and nights at their chosen college and may need to attend as many as four or five subject-specific interviews across the university.

There are some things that you should be prepared for in relation to subject specific interviews.

Reading material

Particularly in arts and humanities subjects, reading material is often given to interviewees an hour prior to a subject-specific interview. For history, for example, you may be given a primary source to analyse. For English, you may be given a poem or a short story to read. For geography you may be given a map or photograph to study. In modern languages you will almost certainly be given some grammar and translation work to do. These tasks will form the first part of the interview, and will give you a chance to prove how well you can think on your feet. In some cases interviewers will even give you additional tasks to do when you are in the room with them.

Questions about your Personal Statement

You can be pretty certain that your interviewer(s) will want to discuss your Personal Statement at some point. They will assume that you will be comfortable talking about anything you mentioned in it. The interviewer may then follow your ideas up with more probing questions.

Problem solving in science subjects and mathematics

In interviews for science subjects and mathematics, a large part of any subject-specific interview will consist of working through problems in front of your interviewer. These will normally start simply and relate closely to your A level syllabus. They will then get progressively harder. Try to apply knowledge from situations you have encountered before to unfamiliar questions, and remember to verbalise your thought processes, particularly if you are stuck.

Interviews in other languages

If you are applying to read modern languages and have studied your chosen language to A level, the interviewer may conduct your discussions in that language. If you hope to study a language from scratch, for example Russian, you will not be expected to speak Russian to your interviewer.

Questions about current affairs

Be up to date with current affairs that relate specifically to your subject. Skim broadsheet newspapers for anything relevant and read recent journal publications in your field if you have access to them. Most things are easily available on the web.

What characteristics are the interviewers looking for?

There are a few absolutely essential characteristics that interviewers will be looking for, some of which you will already have considered when writing your Personal Statement. These include:

1| passion for your subject
2| knowledge of your subject and a very good understanding of the school syllabus (if relevant)
3| the ability to think critically and analytically
4| the ability to think independently
5| 'teachability' (the ability to listen and work well in a supervision setting).

1. Passion for your subject

Having a passion for your subject is possibly the most important thing to get across during an interview

To come this far, you will already have had to prove that you are academically capable. However, it is your excitement about your chosen subject and an enthusiasm to learn more about it that will interest your interviewers. Remember, they will be dedicating their teaching time to you, possibly with an idea to training you up to join their faculty in years to come, and they take their work very seriously. Passion for your subject can be illustrated in a variety of ways.

- Your body language at the interview and the way you communicate with your interviewers: if you smile, talk energetically and enthusiastically, and look interested when they offer their ideas, this will give them the feeling that you are really passionate about the subject.
- If you have read a great deal and are ready to discuss what you have explored with your interviewer, you are obviously seriously interested in your chosen subject.
- If you have taken the time to organise work experience related to your subject and you can discuss this with your interviewer, you will show your commitment to your chosen field.

2. Knowledge of your subject

Knowledge about your subject is often important as a starting point for further study at university, particularly in science subjects.

If you have studied your subject at school, interviewers will expect you to know the syllabus inside out as a starting point for discussion, before pushing you further. Interviewers will find out about your knowledge in several ways.

- They may ask A level syllabus-related questions, such as: 'which module did you enjoy most in history this year?' Make the most of a question like this to really show the interviewer what you know. Rather than giving a one word answer, elaborate and explain why. Go into as much detail as you can.
- In mathematics or science subjects, interviewers will probably give you practical questions to work out. These may start with problems that you have encountered before at school and then progress to harder ones.

3. Critical and analytical thinking

The ability to think critically and analytically is very important at university.

Interviewers want to see that you can play with ideas and make judgements about what you have read. This shows that you can form opinions of your own and are able to organise information into a coherent argument in your head, and then in words. Interviewers can test you on this in several ways.

When interviewing for arts or humanities subjects, interviewers may ask you questions that specifically require you to make judgements and organise your ideas. For example, in an interview to read English they might ask: 'So, what do you think is particularly striking about the war poetry of Wilfred Owen?' A good candidate may perhaps discuss several poems, one by one, pointing out one idea per poem. This would be a narratival approach to the question and would prove that the candidate had good knowledge of the subject, but would not show that they could think critically about it. Better candidates will think about common themes that run through all Owen's war poetry and then consider which theme is the most 'striking'. This candidate would have critically analysed her/his ideas and organised the answer into a coherent argument.

4. Independent thinking

It is also important to show that you can think independently and 'outside the box'. An ability to think around a question shows flair and initiative and is very attractive to interviewers. Particularly in humanities subjects like history and English, undergraduate students are expected to absorb incredible amounts of information through independent reading, without the help of tutors or supervisors. It is therefore very important that you can think and work for yourself. To explore your independence, an interviewer may ask you about a subject which you have never come across before. Interviewers may ask different questions to assess your independence of mind, for example:

- In a mathematics interview, the interviewer may show you a new type of simultaneous equation. You may never have seen this type, but if you attempt to solve it by using the principles you have learnt when tackling simpler problems you will be using your knowledge creatively and independently.
- In a humanities subject, for example history, the interviewer could ask you to discuss the potential causes for an obscure event that you know little or nothing about. In this instance, if you can compare the event to one that you have studied, you may be able to apply your previous knowledge to the new situation. Rather than giving up, you would have shown intellectual courage and lateral thinking.

5. Teachability

Finally, it is very important that the interviewer feels like he or she can imagine teaching you in a small group on a regular basis.

The interview set-up is quite similar to a seminar or tutorial, so if you are accepted, you and your interviewer will be working together like this every week. Much of what will make the interviewer feel comfortable has been said above. If you are passionate, independently minded and have worked hard previously, your interviewer will probably feel you are a worthwhile candidate. However, if you fit with the following criterion, you are probably particularly suited to the tutorial system.

- You feel comfortable discussing your ideas out loud, and are not shy to give your opinions.
- You are also someone who can listen carefully to suggestions, and are able to adapt your opinions in order to take the ideas of the tutors or supervisors on board.

Finally when thinking about what admissions tutors find attractive, it may be useful to consider what they do not want to see. Admissions tutors have said that there are common mistakes or traits that unsuccessful applicants have. Unsuccessful applicants:

- *are too eager to agree/not keen to discuss/debate*
- *are well informed but cautious or uncritical in thinking*
- *had difficulty when challenged to think for self*
- *are reluctant to engage with the unfamiliar*
- *jump into answers without listening.*

Admissions Tutor, Cambridge

Interview styles

'If you could put four things into a space capsule and send it into outer space, what would you chose?'

I was asked this question during a history interview at Cambridge in 2002. Horror stories about unkind Oxbridge interviewers, asking completely random questions, are common. In the newspapers and by word of mouth we are told that we will be asked things that seem totally unrelated to the subject we hope to study. This is, however, uncommon. As an interviewer for history at Oxford says:

This type of question should not be asked and rarely is. We do not want to trick you or to make you look stupid. We simply want to find out how your mind works. If you are asked a strange question, you are well within your rights to ask the interviewer what they mean or want.

Oxford interviewer, 2009

What is clear, however, is that many interviewers do not have any formal training. They are academics, not schoolteachers. They are probably perfectly nice people, but may not be excellent communicators. They are human and make mistakes, and they can often phrase questions unclearly. If this happens, you can ask them to clarify. They may rephrase the question for you, or they may decide not to, and wait to see what you come up with. There are as many different interview styles as there are interviewers, but you can be prepared for some of the tougher ones just in case.

The passive interviewer

This type of interviewer can be the hardest to deal with. It doesn't matter how enthusiastic you are, you just can't get them to seem interested in what you are saying. This can make you feel crushed and unsure about how well you are doing. The only thing you can do in this situation is to keep your head up and carry on going.

Alternatively, the interviewer may seem so laid back that anything you say is acceptable. This can be dangerous. Whereas a pushy interviewer will put pressure on you to find the right answer or develop your argu-. ment, the laid back interviewers will not. They may either be happy with one-word answers from you, talking endlessly themselves, or they may let you rabbit away without giving you any direction. Either way, it is hard to show your full potential in this sort of situation. If this happens, you need to be very aware of the length of your answers. Try to expand your responses so that you show the breadth of your knowledge, but do not talk for too long. Your answers should never continue for more than one minute without input from your interviewer.

Don't be fooled by a passive or relaxed interviewer. Just because they are reclining in their chair does not mean you can lie back in yours. Remember, you are performing. Keep your mind clearly focused on the task at hand.

The aggressive interviewer

A brutal interview can be a terrifying experience and can make the most confident candidates quake in their seats. First of all, keep a clear head and never take anything personally. A good intellectual argument can be a very attractive thing to an academic. One of the common features of this interview style is the oft repeated question 'And????'. Whatever you say, however you develop your argument, the interviewer exclaims, 'and?' at the end of your answer, before you have a chance to gasp for breath. When faced with this situation, keep thinking around the sub-ject. You can say, 'Well, I am not sure, but you could look at it like this: . . . '. or 'I guess an alternative angle might be . . . '. Keep going and keep thinking. If you have exhausted all the possibilities that you can think of, a good way to give in is: 'I really can't think of anything else, but I would really love to find out. Could you tell me?' You will appear interested and this is a key factor in the make-up of a good candidate. The interviewer may well have a very specific answer in mind that you could not have possibly guessed. However, in these situations, the pro-cess is often more important than the solution. Remember, they want to find out how your mind works, not just what you know.

Aggressive interviewers may ask you obscure questions that seem to be intended purely to catch you out. At all times, especially when unsure about the question, verbalise your thought processes. It is always a good idea to stop and think for a few seconds before launching into an answer. Once you have thought about one point you could say: 'I haven't thought about this before, but it seems similar to . . . '. If you do not understand the question, ask the interviewer to clarify. Be up-front and open.

An interviewer may also play devil's advocate and argue with you just for the sake of it. He or she will be testing your ability to formulate a strong argument and to stick by it. When discussing contentious issues, make sure not to generalise. Always think of some empirical data or detailed proof to back up your judgement. In this way you will strengthen your argument and make it harder for the interviewer to back you into a corner. In a heated discussion, don't be afraid to follow through with your ideas to the end. Take care, however, if things get too heated, to back down gracefully. Your interviewer will have been working in his or her field probably since before you were born, and is likely to know what they are talking about.

The scribbler

In some interviews there will be more than one interviewer. Often, in this situation, one person will talk and another will scribble down notes. It may be disconcerting watching someone 'marking' your performance in front of you, and you may feel unsure about whom to address your answers to. The best course of action is to ignore the second person as much as possible. Listen to the interviewer who speaks, and then respond to him/her. Of course, include the other interviewer if he or she looks up, but don't feel you need to wait for a response from them before continuing with your discussion.

■ Interview questions

It is a very good idea to predict the questions you might be asked at interview and practise working through your responses. An obvious place to start is your Personal Statement. Your interviewers are likely to have this on the table in front of them during the interview, and will have skimmed through it immediately before you arrive. This will be used as a starting point for discussion. They are likely to pick up on any books and articles you have mentioned or subjects you say you particularly enjoyed at school. Make sure you have reread everything you mention in your Personal Statement, and are ready to discuss your ideas about them.

Below are lists of questions that have come up in previous years.

General interview questions
- Why do you want to come to this college?
- What made you want to study this subject?
- What are you intending to do in your gap year?
- Where do you see yourself in five years' time?
- Excluding your A level reading, what were the last three books you read?
- What do you regard as your strengths and weaknesses?
- What extra-curricular activities would you like to take part in at this college?

- Why did you make an 'open application'?
- Give us three reasons why we should offer you a place.
- What will you do if we don't?
- Why did you chose your A level subjects?
- How will this degree help in your chosen career?
- How would your friends describe you?
- Why are you having to retake your A level(s)? What happened last year?

Subject-specific interview questions

Anthropology/archaeology

- Name the six major world religions.
- What does Stonehenge mean to you?
- What are the problems regarding objectivity in anthropological studies?
- Why do civilisations erect monuments?
- Why should we approach all subjects from a holistic, anthropological perspective?

Art history

- What do we look for when we study art? What are we trying to reveal?
- Comment on this painting on the wall.
- Compare and contrast these three images.
- What exhibitions have you been to recently?
- How can you determine whether a piece of art is successful or not?/ how do you determine the value of art?
- Who should own art?
- What is art?
- Why is art important?
- What role do art galleries and museums play in society today?
- Are humans inherently creative?
- Apart from your studies, how else might you pursue your interest in art history while at the university?
- What are some key themes in the history of art?
- How has the depiction of the human form developed through the centuries?
- Who invented linear perspective, artists or architects?

Biochemistry

- How do catalysts work?
- Describe the work of enzymes.
- Discuss the chemistry of the formation of proteins.
- Questions on oxidation, equilibria and interatomic forces.
- Questions on X-ray crystallography.
- Why do you wish to read biochemistry rather than chemistry?

■ What scientific journals have you read lately? Is there a recent development in the field that particularly interests you?

Biological sciences

■ How does the immune system recognise invading pathogens as foreign cells?
■ How does a cell stop itself from exploding due to osmosis?
■ Why is carbon of such importance in living systems?
■ How would you transfer a gene to a plant?
■ Explain the mechanism of capillary action.
■ What are the advantages of the human genome project?
■ How would you locate a gene for a given characteristic in the nucleus of a cell?
■ What is the major problem with heart transplants in the receiver?
■ How does the transplant receiver respond to foreign heart cells?
■ How does the body recognise and distinguish its own cells from the foreign cells after a transplant?

Chemistry

■ Questions on organic mechanisms.
■ Questions on structure, bonding and energetics.
■ Questions on acids and bases.
■ Questions on isomerisation.
■ Questions on practical chemical analysis.

(See also biochemistry questions.)

Classics

■ Questions on classical civilisations and literature.
■ Why do you think ancient history is important?
■ How civilised was the Roman world?
■ Apart from your A level texts, what have you read in the original or in translation?

Earth sciences and geology

■ Where would you place this rock sample in geological time?
■ How would you determine a rock's age?
■ Can you integrate this decay curve, and why would the result be useful?
■ Questions on chemistry.
■ When do you think oil will run out?

Economics

■ Explain how the Phillips curve arises.
■ Would it be feasible to have an economy which was entirely based on the service sector?
■ A man pays for his holiday at a hotel on a tropical island by cheque. He has a top credit rating and rather than cashing it, the hotelier

pays a supplier using the same cheque. That supplier does the same thing with one of his suppliers and so on ad infinitum. Who pays for the man's holiday?

- What do you know about the interaction between fiscal and monetary policy?
- I notice that you study mathematics. Can you see how you might derive the profit maximisation formula from first principles?
- Tell me about competition in the television industry.
- How effective is current monetary policy?
- What are your particular interests as regards economics?
- Do you think we should worry about a balance of payments deficit?
- If you were the Chancellor of the Exchequer, how would you maximise tax revenue?
- If you had a fairy godmother who gave you unlimited sums of money, what sort of company would you start and what types of employee would you hire?
- What are the advantages and disadvantages of joining the euro?
- What are the qualities of a good economist?
- Why are you studying Economics A level?
- What would happen to employment and wage rates if the pound depreciated?
- Do you the think the Chinese exchange rate will increase?
- How does the housing market affect inflation?
- How has social mobility changed in recent times?

Engineering

- Questions on mathematics and physics, particularly calculus and mechanics.
- Questions on mathematical derivations, for example, of laws of motion.
- This mechanical system sitting on my desk – how does it work?
- How do aeroplanes fly?
- What is impedance matching and how can it be achieved?
- How do bicycle spokes work?
- How would you divide a tetrahedron into two identical parts?
- What is the total resistance of the tetrahedron if there are resistors of one ohm on each edge?
- Questions on Hooke's law.

English

- What defines a novel as Gothic?
- What is the most important work of literature of the twentieth century?
- Who is your favourite author?
- Do you do any creative writing? Do you keep a diary? Do you write letters?

- Apart from your A level texts, what three books have you read recently?
- Give a review of the last Shakespeare play you saw at the theatre.
- What do you think about the hypothesis that Shakespeare was unusually atheistic for his time?
- Critically analyse this poem.
- How has the author used language in this text?
- Are Iago and Othello good listeners?

Geography

- Is geography just a combination of other disciplines?
- Why should it be studied in its own right?
- Would anything remain of geography if we took the notion of place off the syllabus?
- How important is the history of towns when studying settlement patterns?
- Why is climate so unpredictable?
- What is the importance of space in global warming?
- Why do you think people care about human geography more than physical geography?
- What is more important, mapping or computer models?
- If you went to an isolated island to do research on the beach how would you use the local community?
- Analyse a graph about a river. Why are there peaks and troughs?
- Look at a world map showing quality of life indicators. Explain the pattern in terms of two of the indicators.

(See also questions on land economy.)

History

- Discuss an historical movement that you find particularly interesting.
- How can one define revolution?
- Why did imperialism happen?
- Who was the greater democrat – Gladstone or Disraeli?
- Was the fall of the Weimar Republic inevitable?
- 'History is the study of the present with the benefit of hindsight.' Do you agree?
- Would history be worth studying if it didn't repeat itself?
- What is the difference between modern history and modern politics?
- What is the position of the individual in history?
- Would you abolish the monarchy for ideological or practical reasons?
- Should we abolish the House of Lords?
- Should we elect the second chamber?
- Why do historians differ in their views on Hitler?
- What skills should a historian have?

- In what periods has the Holy Grail been popular, with whom and why?
- Why do you think the Holy Grail gains more attention during certain periods?
- Why is it important to visit historical sites relevant to the period you are studying?

Human sciences

- Talk about bovine spongiform encephalopathy and its implications, and the role of prions in Creutzfeldt–Jakob disease.
- What causes altitude sickness and how do humans adapt physiologically to high altitudes?
- Tell me about the exploitation of indigenous populations by Westerners.
- Why is statistics a useful subject for human scientists?
- Why are humans so difficult to experiment with?
- How would you design an experiment to determine whether genetics or upbringing is more important?
- What are the scientific implications of globalisation on the world?

Land economy

- Will the UK lose its sovereignty if it joins EMU?
- Will EMU encourage regionalism?
- Will the information technology revolution gradually result in the death of inner cities?
- What has been the effect of the Channel tunnel on surrounding land use?

Law

- Questions on the points of law arising from scenarios – often relating to criminal law or duty of care.
- A cyclist rides the wrong way down a one-way street and a chimney falls on him. What legal proceedings should he take? What if he is riding down a private drive signed 'no trespassing'?
- X intends to poison his wife but accidentally gives the lethal draught to her identical twin. Would you consider this a murder?
- Questions on legal issues, particularly current ones.
- Should stalking be a criminal offence?
- Should judges have a legislative role?
- Do you think that anyone should be able to serve on a jury?
- Should judges be elected?
- Do judges have political bias?
- To what extent do you think the press should be able to release information concerning allegations against someone?
- Is there anything you want to discuss or that you're really interested in?
- Who do you think has the right to decide about euthanasia?

- How does the definition of intent distinguish murder from man-slaughter?
- Can you give definitions of murder and manslaughter?
- Should foresight of consequences be considered as intending such consequences?

Material sciences

- Questions on physics, particularly solid materials.
- Questions on mathematics, particularly forces.
- Investigations of sample materials, particularly structure and fractures.

Maths and computation

- Questions (which may become progressively harder) on almost any area of the A level syllabus.

Maths and further maths

- Pure maths questions on integration.
- Applied maths questions on forces.
- Statistics questions on probability.
- Computation questions on iterations, series and computer arithmetic.

Medicine

- What did your work experience teach you about life as a doctor?
- What did you learn about asthma in your work experience on asthma research?
- How have doctors' lives changed in the past 30 years?
- Explain the logic behind the most recent NHS reforms.
- What are the mechanisms underlying diabetes?
- Why is it that cancer cells are more susceptible to destruction by radiation than normal cells?
- How would you determine whether leukaemia patients have con-tracted the disease because of a nearby nuclear power station?
- What does isometric exercise mean in the context of muscle function?
- What can you tell me about the mechanisms underlying sensory adaptation?
- What is an ECG?
- Why might a general practitioner not prescribe antibiotics to a toddler?
- Why are people anxious before surgery? Is it justifiable?
- How do you deal with stress?
- Questions on gene therapy.
- Questions on the ethics of fetal transplantation.
- Questions on biochemistry and human biology.

Modern languages

- Tests and questions on comprehension and translation.
- Reading tests.
- Questions which focus on the use of language in original texts.

- Describe aspects of this poem which you find interesting.
- Interpret this poem, commenting about the tone and the context of the poem.
- Why do you want to study your language and not another?
- Why is it important to study literature?
- What is the difference between literature and philosophy?
- What French book have you recently read that you enjoyed?
- French conversation – talking about a work placement.
- Questions on cultural and historical context and genre in European literature.
- How important is analysis of narrative in the study of literature?
- How important is biography in the study of literature?

Natural sciences

- What is an elastic collision?
- What happens when two particles collide – one moving and one stationary?
- What is friction?
- Questions on carboxylic acids.

Oriental studies

- What do you know about the Chinese language and its structure?
- What are the differences between English and any Oriental language with which you are familiar?
- Compare and contrast any ambiguities in the following sentences.
  - Only suitable magazines are sold here.
  - Many species inhabit a small space.
  - He is looking for the man who crashed his car.
- Comment on the following sentences.
  - He did wrong.
  - He was wrong.
  - He was about to do wrong.

Philosophy

- What is philosophy?
- What philosophical questions have you come across?
- Would you agree that if p is true and s believes p, then s knows p?
- Was the question you have just answered about knowing or about the meaning of the word 'know'?
- Comment on these statements/questions.
  - I could be dreaming that I am in this interview./I do not know whether I am dreaming or not./Therefore I do not know whether I am in this interview or not.
  - A machine has a free will.
  - When I see red, could I be seeing what you see when you see green?

- Is it a matter of fact or logic that time travels in one direction only?
- Is our faith in scientific method itself based on scientific method? If so, does it matter?
- I can change my hairstyle and still be me. I can change my political opinions and still be me. I can have a sex change and still be me. What is it then that makes me be me?
- Can it ever be morally excusable to kill someone?

Physics

- Questions on applied mathematics.
- Questions on any aspect of the physics syllabus.
- Questions on mathematical derivations.
- How does glass transmit light?
- How does depressing a piano key make a sound?
- How does the voltage on a capacitor vary if the dielectric gas is ionised?

Politics

- Can you define 'government'? Why do we need governments?
- Can you differentiate between power and authority?
- How can you distinguish between a society, a state and an economy?
- Will Old Labour ever be revived? If so, under what circumstances?
- Why do you think that Communism was unsuccessful in the Russian countryside?
- What would you say to someone who claims that women already have equal opportunities?
- What would you do tomorrow if you were the president of the former Soviet Union?
- How does a democracy work?
- What constitute the ideologies of the extreme right?
- Does the extreme right pose a threat to other less extreme parties?
- What do you think of Labour's discrimination in favour of female parliamentarians?
- How would you improve the comprehensive system of education?

Politics, philosophy and economics

- Define 'power', 'authority' and 'influence'.
- How important is national identity? What is the Scottish national identity?
- Should medics pay more for their degrees?
- Can you point out the difference in the mentality of Americans in 1760 and 1770?

Psychology

- Questions on neurophysiology.
- Questions on statistics.

- Questions on the experimental elucidation of the mechanisms underlying behaviour.
- Give some examples of why an understanding of chemistry might be important in psychology.
- A new treatment is tested on a group of depressives, who are markedly better in six weeks. Does this show that the treatment was effective?
- There are records of violent crimes that exactly mimic scenes of violence on television. Does this indicate that television causes real violence?
- How would you establish the quietest sound that you can hear as opposed to the quietest sound that you think you can hear?
- Why might one be able to remember items at the beginning and end of an aurally presented list better than items in the middle?
- Could a computer ever feel emotion?
- Is it ethically justifiable to kill animals for the purpose of research?
- What is emotional intelligence?

Social and political sciences

- What is the value of the study of social anthropology?
- Do people need tabloids?
- How would you define terrorism?
- Do you believe in selective education? Are we participating in selective education here?
- Is it possible to pose a sociological problem without sociological bias?
- Does prison work?
- Are MPs only in it for the power?
- What aspects of the subject are you particularly looking forward to studying?

(See also questions on politics.)

Theology

- Does moral rectitude reside in the agent, the act or its consequences?
- What, if anything, is wrong with voluntary euthanasia?
- What is the best reason that you can think of for believing in the existence of God?
- Do you think that this course could conceivably be persuasive on the issue?
- What relevance does theology have for art history?
- What relevance does archaeology have for theology?
- Can you comment on the portrayal of Jesus in John versus the other gospels?

Veterinary medicine

- Should the veterinary profession show positive discrimination in favour of men?

- Has your work experience influenced your future career aspirations?
- Can you discuss any aspect of animal physiology which has struck you as contrasting with what you know of human physiology.
- Would our knowledge of BSE have been of value in controlling foot and mouth disease?
- Tell me about the biochemistry of DNA.
- What animal did this skull belong to?

(See also questions on biological sciences and chemistry.)

Any questions?

At the end of the interview you may be asked if you have any questions to ask the interviewer(s). It is always a good idea to have a few questions up your sleeve. One or two is a good number; more than three questions is usually too many. Write them down on a notepad and bring it with you. You will appear professional and keen. You may be able to bring up one of your favourite topics that was not discussed during the main part of the interview. If, after all your research, you still have questions about your course or college, this is the time to ask. If there was a topic covered during the interview that you didn't understand, you could enquire about where you can read more about it, or get further clarification from the interviewers themselves.

Interview stories from previous applicants

Adam, Economics, Cambridge

Two weeks before my interview I was sent an interview pack from Cambridge, which contained an article that I read in advance of the interview, a few maps of the college and of Cambridge, some information about the interviews and a food voucher for the food hall.

My interview was at midday. I could have stayed over the night before but I live close so I didn't. There were no designated student helpers and I got a bit lost in the college (it is very large) so I asked some people for help and directions. I would recommend going to the porter's lodge if you get very lost and they will direct you.

My first interview was the specialist interview for economics. I was interviewed by two fellows, who invited me to sit down on a couch as I entered the room where the interview took place. One interviewer sat directly in front of me and the other sat at a desk looking to the side. The interviewer who sat in front of me was the main interviewer, as the other interviewer hardly ever intervened and just took notes. The interview started with the principal interviewer asking me about what current events in the news had interested me most. I responded by talking about Northern Rock. She asked me why I was interested in what was happening at the time with Northern Rock. I told her that it stemmed from my great interest in economics and related it to out-of-class reading I had done on banking systems. The interview continued in that same tone and style. It was a very sober, tense environment. The interview was very formal and no time was lost on discussions that did not relate to economics.

I was sent an article a couple of weeks prior to the interview. And I was asked a few questions on it. The answers basically related back to my A level knowledge of the subject. Then I was given a paragraph on economics and was told to comment on it. The comment could be anything I wanted to say or thought about the paragraph. It had some errors, that were not grammatical; it rested on dubious theory such as 'if you raise taxes, people will spend more', whereas I have been taught that if you raise taxes people will spend less.

Then they asked me a mathematical problem. They gave me a whiteboard to solve it on. It was a geometric problem. The problem was that there were two pieces of carpet and you had to cover an entire room with those two pieces of carpet. The trick was you could only make one cut. This seemed to me to be impossible. I was told to do what I could and I talked through the logic of finding the solution to the problem. I was stopped after around 30 seconds. After the maths question, the interviewers asked me if I had any questions. I asked them about fiscal policy and we had a short discussion and then the interview came to an end.

My general interview was very relaxed. The admissions tutor asked me questions such as 'Why Cambridge?', 'Why this college?' and 'Tell me five words your friends would use to describe you'. I was also told to describe an object as if I was on the telephone with the admissions tutor and they could not see the object. After I described the object, he asked me why I thought he had asked that question. This laid-back style characterised the interview. It was quite an enjoyable experience. The interviewer's questions were either very general and expected or very diverse, unusual and startling.

Melissa, Human Sciences, Oxford

I had two interviews which seemed to me more like discussions than any sort of interrogation. I had done a mock interview in order to prepare and I was pleased that I had, because its style had prepared me for the worst! When I arrived, the undergraduates at the college were incredibly helpful, as they were able to give me an insight into what my interviewers were like, and they told me what little they could remember of their own interviews too.

The first interview lasted around 30 minutes and took place in an office just big enough for the two of us. The interviewer started by telling me about himself and some recent research he had been doing – I was so shocked by this because I had expected everything to be about me! It calmed me down, though, because it was like an ordinary conversation. He then started to ask me why I had chosen this subject over others that might have seemed more obvious for someone with my A levels. We then moved on to some technical questions. For one I had to comment on a graph showing the typical age when people die in certain countries. As I had not looked at this beforehand I had to think on my feet.

My interviewer had looked at the work I had sent in, and asked me to look at how one of the essays related to the subject I was applying for. He let me talk on about this for what seemed like ages and asked me lots of things about it. He seemed interested but I couldn't really tell what he thought of me.

In the second interview, I felt far more challenged but not in a confrontational way. When I was asked a question and gave an answer the interviewer would ask me yet another question on my answer. A common question she asked was 'Why?'. It was a very exciting interview and she seemed genuinely interested in what I had to say. Although I think I tackled a lot of it well on my own, she often prompted me to get me thinking along the right lines.

Both the interviewers were very friendly and seemed to be keen to find my strengths rather than my weaknesses. On the whole, I suppose, I actually enjoyed the experience!

Grace, History, Oxford

When I arrived at Oxford for the interview I was terribly nervous. I was taken through to a small study where two female professors were sitting. As soon as I walked in, I could sense that the atmosphere was much more relaxed than I had imagined it would be. The initial questions they asked me were drawn from points I had made in my Personal Statement, many of them about the Holy Grail. This immediately made me feel more relaxed, as I was confident about being able to support what I had written in my Personal Statement.

It was clear to me that they were not trying to trick me by asking questions about historical periods I hadn't covered. They were far more interested in the periods I had covered and were trying to engage me in debate by contradicting a number of the arguments I put forward.

After around 20 minutes, the questions became focused on an essay I had submitted prior to the interview. The questions were designed to make me look at alternative arguments to those I had used in my essay, and they made me question whether my arguments were right. However, when one of the interviewers asked me a question that seemed to have numerous correct answers, I realised that they were more interested in my ability to analyse different points of view.

I enjoyed my interview but I was not offered a place.

Imogen, French and Italian, Oxford

I was called for an interview about 10 days before the provisional date, but the letter did nothing except confirm that I had been called. There were no times or details given. Upon arrival at Oxford, the night before the interviews began, I learnt that the next day I had a language test and an Italian interview, and a French interview the following day.

Oxford prefers not to allow candidates to make their own way to interviews, in case they get lost, so each college has a general waiting room and a group of current undergraduate helpers to accompany everyone. On the morning of the test, all the modern linguists gathered in the waiting room, and we were shown to classrooms where we had to take a grammar test in each of the languages we were applying for, except those we were intending to study from scratch. I sat tests in French and Italian, lasting an hour in total, and consisting of translation and multiple choice questions.

My Italian interview took place at Balliol (I applied to St Anne's), because there is no Italian fellow at St Anne's. A student helper took me to Balliol, and I was given an Italian poem to look at. This was discussed in my interview and I was then asked to talk about subjects I had brought up in my Personal Statement. We then discussed various books I had read and, surprisingly, did not speak any Italian.

I had one interviewer for first the Italian interview. This was a very strange interview. I was given an Italian poem ('Canzonetta sulle sirene catodiche' by Magrelli) to read and make notes on before I was called in.

- I had to describe aspects of the poem which I found interesting.
- I was then asked to summarise my Personal Statement as he hadn't seen it before.
- Then he asked me why I thought that Primo Levi was a good writer, told me that his book was originally rejected by Natalia Ginzburg and asked what I felt about that.
- The conversation then moved on to Dante, and he wanted to know how I had approached my study of 'L'Inferno', and which of the 'canti' I had enjoyed.
- I was then given the opportunity to ask him a question.

The second part of the interview consisted of a discussion of a poem and I had two interviewers. When I met the interviewers they gave me a poem to read in English.

- Again, the poem was discussed in depth, but this time I was pushed to interpret bits which were harder to understand, rather than just comment on bits I liked.
- The interviewer then picked up on the Primo Levi in my Personal Statement, and asked me what I thought of the quote 'After Auschwitz, no more poetry', with reference to the philosophy I studied at school.

- There was a brief conversation in Italian, focusing on current affairs and places I had visited in Italy.
- Again I was allowed to ask a question.

The next morning I had a French interview at St Anne's. Again I was given a passage to read, again in English, which was discussed with one of the interviewers.

There was a conversation in French with a second interviewer, which covered some literature and my reasons for studying French. Lastly, the third interviewer asked some slightly more in-depth questions about the importance of literature, and the relationship between literature and philosophy (I had made some references to philosophy in my Personal Statement).

I had three interviewers for my first French interview. I was given another passage in English; it was an extract from the works of Edgar Allen Poe.

- I was asked questions about the tone of the passage, what situation I thought the extract was taken from and how I felt the episode would conclude.
- Then we had a conversation in French – why I wanted to study French as opposed to any other language, what I felt the themes were in the film *Jules et Jim* by Francois Truffaut (the essay I sent up was based on this film) and what I felt the film said about the difference between the French and the Germans during the war.
- I was asked a series of questions, including: Why is it important to study literature? What is the difference between literature and philosophy? What French book had I recently read that I enjoyed? I talked about 'La Princesse de Cleves'.

My second interview for French had two interviewers. This time I was given a poem to read in French. There was a note at the top saying that I should try to understand the poem, but not worry if I didn't know all the vocabulary, because I would be asked which bits of the poem I found most interesting and was not expected to understand it all.

- However, I was then fired a series of questions on every verse of the poem, and interrupted during every answer to be further questioned on why I thought that, where I was getting my information from, and could I give more examples to back up my point. Luckily, I had been placed in a library to read through the passage, and so had looked up all the unfamiliar vocabulary. The moral of the story – don't believe the kindly worded instructions!
- One of the interviewers then said he was intrigued as to my interest in Ronsard, and we discussed where the major Petrarchian influences were in the poetry.
- Then followed a French conversation where I had to talk about my work placement in Le Touquet, and what I thought the differences were between French and British holidaymakers.

I had been told that I would be allowed to leave Oxford at 10 a.m. the following morning, but that some candidates would be required to stay until later the next day to attend interviews at other colleges.

Madeleine, Modern and Medieval Languages, Cambridge

Shortly after I had sent off my UCAS form, Cambridge contacted me by letter to give me details of the written work they required, which in my case was two essays; one for Latin and one for Italian. I wrote an essay in English for the Latin requirement, and a short essay based on an A level topic in Italian. These essays were due early in November.

I was then called to interview, again by letter, which arrived roughly half-way through November, and was told all the details and times of the tests and interviews I would be expected to sit, which all took place on one day in the first half of December.

I stayed in college the night before my interviews, due to an early start the next day, which I would highly recommend as it gives one the opportunity to get used to the surroundings, talk to current students and it means that it isn't a great rush in the morning before the interview. I had to sit a test first, and as a language applicant I had to choose one of my languages in which to answer. In my case, it had to be Italian, but as it turned out, very little of the test was actually in the foreign language. There was a passage to be read, in English, which I had to summarise in a foreign language (Italian), and then I had to answer a very broad essay question in English. The test lasted an hour.

My first interview was a couple of hours later, so I took the opportunity to have lunch with some friends who were also applying to other colleges, whilst making sure I left myself plenty of time to get to the interview, which was for the Latin side of my application. I was given some Latin poetry to read, try to understand and analyse, and this was then discussed in the interview. I was also questioned about the essay I had sent up, and was given some general questions about why I had applied for the course and what my gap year plans were. In this particular interview, there were two interviewers.

Following this was my Italian interview, which was conducted by one person only. Again, I was given a passage to try to understand and talk about, and then we discussed the literature that I was studying for my A2. Finally, she asked me a couple of questions in Italian to test my standard of speaking, focusing on where I had visited in Italy.

After this, I was free to leave, with nothing else to do but wait for the result. At Cambridge the results are all given out on one day, shortly after Christmas, and this date is stated in advance. There will be one of three possible results given on this day, either an acceptance, a rejection or the news that you have been placed in the 'winter pool', which means that there is a possibility that another college will accept you, based on the strength of your UCAS form. Acceptance or rejection from this pool can be held until as late as the end of January, during which time there is the possibility of being called for further interviewing.

John, Modern and Medieval Languages (Latin), Cambridge

I was given a 20-line passage of Ovid's *Metamorphoses*, about half an hour before the start of the interview, and left in the library to look at it. I was then taken to the interview room. I was addressed first by the general admissions tutor for Modern and Medieval Languages, who asked me what had brought me to my choice of languages (Latin and Italian), and which aspects of the course at Cambridge appealed. She then asked me lots of questions about the gap year I intended to take, how I thought it would be beneficial to me and how I planned to keep my study skills alive whilst I was away.

The rest of the interview was taken by the Latin lecturer, who started by asking me some grammatical questions about the passage I had looked at. I had to translate bits of it, and then identify some literary techniques used. We then talked about the passage in general, about the themes and general storyline.

The interviewer then brought up the essay I had sent, which was an analysis of Book I of Virgil's *Aeneid*. He questioned me quite intensely on one comment I had made, until I couldn't defend myself any longer.

We discussed my Personal Statement, in particular the references I had made to Linear B, an ancient Mycenaean language, and I was asked what reading I had done to develop this unusual interest. Last, he asked me to imagine that I was talking to someone who had never studied classics before, and to recommend them one book to read and explain my choice.

■ Presentation skills: making an impression without words

It is widely agreed amongst psychologists today that we make powerful impressions on other people simply through our physical appearance and body language. In fact some say that body language counts for over 90% of the first impression you make.

Going for interview is stressful and it would be strange if you were not a little nervous. But don't be afraid of your nerves. Use them to heighten your awareness of the way you move, speak and engage with the interviewer(s). Below are some suggestions from John Meeske, a psychologist at the MPW school.

- First, always carry yourself well, especially when you first enter the room; hold your head high, stand up straight, and smile.

- Shake the interviewer's hand firmly (without hurting them) and make direct eye contact. We often look to see where to shake and forget to make eye-contact at all.

Interviews will generally be conducted in the offices of a potential direc-tor of studies or tutor. These studies are often a part-way between a living room and an office. You may be asked to settle on a comfortable arm chair or sofa but end up sinking down into it. Alternatively you may be given a hard backed chair to sit on and find yourself perching on the edge. Whichever it is, John Meeske advises:

- take a moment to accustom yourself to the chair; you don't want to feel uncomfortable for the whole interview
- lean forward slightly in the chair when you are spoken to; this gives the impression that you are interested and engaged
- put anything you are holding down; this will prevent you from fiddling and will allow you to give your full attention to the interviewer.

If you are asked tricky questions or feel intimidated by your interviewer you may feel unsure about how to respond. But remember, the *way* you say something is often as important as *what* you say. Remain calm and leave a few seconds before you attempt an answer. Whilst you are thinking, look away from the interviewer briefly, to steady your thoughts. When you are ready, bring your eyes back to the interviewer. John Meeske suggests that you:

- maintain good eye-contact with anyone who addresses you, but be sure to use your gaze to invite others present to engage with your responses
- you can also use arm gestures to emphasise your points.

Even if the interview doesn't go as well as you wished, leave with poise. Hold your head high, smile and remember to thank the interviewers for their time. Your first and last impressions will resonate strongly.

Dress relatively smartly to show that you are taking the process seri-ously, and to mentally prepare for this important event. If suits are not your style, however, don't feel you need to buy one. You must simply look presentable, clean and tidy. For boys, a smart pair of trousers or cords, clean shoes and a shirt are suitable. Girls: a smart skirt (no shorter than knee-length) or trousers and a modest top are suitable. Remember, your clothes should not speak more loudly than you.

The pooling system

The pooling system exists to ensure that all strong candidates get a good chance of being accepted to an Oxbridge college, but it means something slightly differently in Cambridge and Oxford.

At Cambridge, pooling happens after the first interview process. If you are a strong candidate, but there has been particularly high competition for places at your college, your interviewers may feel that they cannot offer you a place with them, but that you deserve a place at Cambridge. They will then place you in the 'pool', a database that can be accessed by members of their faculty at different colleges. Academics at these other colleges, who may have spare places or weaker candidates, will then 'fish out' their choice of strong 'pooled' students and ask them to come for interviews at their college. These 'second round' or 'pooling' interviews take place at the college of the academic who selects you, sometime in the second part of December and a few weeks after the first round of interviews. If you are 'pooled' you still stand a chance of being accepted. Around 3,000 offers are made by preference colleges, 600–700 offers are made through the pool.

At Oxford, 'pooling' happens at the same time as the first round interviews. This is the reason Oxford keeps applicants for several days during the interview process. You may be seen by other members of the faculty at different colleges during your stay. If you are a particularly strong candidate, academics at several colleges might ask you to interview, even if they are not at the college of your first choice and even if the academics at your preferred college already know they want to offer you a place. Whereas at Cambridge, being asked to a second round of interviews usually means you have not secured a place at your preferred college, at Oxford more interviews may mean the opposite. This also means that, whereas in Cambridge you will be sent home swiftly and then called up later, at Oxford students may be kept hanging around for several days at a time whilst the academics battle things out between themselves.

06 Getting the letter
Offer or rejection
and how to cope

Once you have had your interview, you may have to wait several weeks before you hear the result. If you applied to Oxford you may hear before Christmas, but you will normally hear from Cambridge in early January. If the college wants to accept you, you will normally get a 'conditional offer'. This is an offer on the condition that you meet the required grades in your A levels. Your place, therefore, will only be confirmed on results day in August. The offer may be 'general', for example, AAB, or 'specific', where the college asks for an A in a particular subject. Most colleges make a standard offer of AAA and a few may make an offer of AAB. Some will stipulate that you need to get 90% in certain A level modules.

A firm or 'unconditional offer' will be made only if you already have your A level grades, for example, if you have taken a gap year. This means you definitely have a place.

If you are unsuccessful, you will receive a rejection letter in the post between December and mid-January. If this is the case for you, do not despair. Remember that there is incredibly high competition to get a place at Oxbridge. Although for many subjects one in six students interviewed are accepted, for others 80 students are interviewed for one place. More than 5,000 of the unsuccessful applicants per year will have been predicted three As at A level, and are clearly intelligent and successful students.

If you are rejected and want to know why, ring the admissions tutor at your chosen college and ask for feedback. If you are really set on claiming a place at Oxbridge, think about why you did not succeed the first time, and try again. Neither Cambridge nor Oxford look badly on students who apply twice. You may have been too young the first time or too focused on school exams to dedicate enough time to the application process. Alternatively, you may not have made an appropriate subject choice and were not passionate enough about your field. If once was enough, however, focus on your other university choices and draw on your Oxbridge experiences to help you in your preparation for future interviews. If you are a motivated and focused student, then you will excel at whatever university you go to, and if you love your subject, then your passion will continue wherever you are.

One of the most compelling reasons to apply to Oxford or Cambridge is because you are excited at the prospect of being taught a subject which you love by people who are at the top of their field in that subject. Remember that you can still have this at another university. If your motivations are like those I've described, you will not be heartbroken but will still look forward avidly to being taught your subject by specialists in another top university. If you do feel unhappy, and it's understandable to feel this way for a short time, speak to your friends, family and teachers to discuss your feelings and get a sense of perspective. Most students feel a bit glum for a while and then look forward to attending their new university.

A word on stress

The whole process of applying to Oxford and Cambridge is very stressful, and you need to be prepared for this, knowing that it is difficult for everyone. Taking A levels is intense and requires incredible stamina and concentration; you are not only competing against your peers, but your strength of character is tried. With your university application riding on the need for particularly good grades, you will probably put even more pressure on yourself than other students. Then there is the UCAS form to complete, the word-perfect Personal Statement that has to be checked and checked again, and the experience of having to defend your ideas against academics who may seem like intellectual giants at interview. There is also the fear of rejection.

However, don't let this put you off. If you learn to compete against yourself, and to love the process of studying, and if you have a real fascination for the subject you wish to study, you will be able to deal with the competition at Oxbridge. If you don't get a place, you will have found a subject that you really enjoy, and this will be an immense advantage, whichever university you go to.

Of course, taking regular breaks from study and discussing your fears with friends can be helpful, and at university students spend a lot of time comparing their workload with their peers and commiserating with each other. A good moan can often do wonders. Taking regular exercise, getting enough sleep, and keeping a circle of trusted friends around you can be very important when coping with stress. You should also remember that, if you are offered a place, the admissions tutors clearly believe you can cope, so you should believe it too! Have faith in yourself. If you don't get an offer, remember, there are many other universities that have world-renowned research departments, and that may offer you a more healthy work–life balance!

Appendix 1: timetables

■ The year before you apply

March

- Request an undergraduate prospectus and the alternative prospectus from the student unions of Cambridge or Oxford.
- Book a place at an open day.
- Research other universities to which you are considering applying (you need to choose four).

April

- Write the first draft of your Personal Statement.
- Go on an open day.

June

- Sit your A levels.

Summer holidays

- Ask friends and family to read your Personal Statement and make revisions.
- Work experience.

■ The year in which you apply

September

- Finalise your Personal Statement with your teachers.
- Visit the UCAS website (www.ucas.com) and register (get a user-name and password).
- Fill in the UCAS form (UCAS applications may be submitted from 1 September).
- Register and book a place to sit the LNAT (if you want to study law at Oxford).
- Register for the BMAT exam if you are applying for medicine (at Oxford or Cambridge) or veterinary science (Cambridge only).

October

- The deadline for UCAS receiving your application form, whether for Oxford or Cambridge, is 15 October.
- Fill in the separate Cambridge Supplementary Application Questionnaire. This will be emailed to you and must be completed by 31 October.

Late October

- Receive acknowledgement letter from your chosen college.
- HAT (for history applicants to Oxford).
- Physics and maths for physics aptitude test (for physics or physics and philosophy applicants to Oxford).
- ELAT (for applicants to English at Oxford).
- Maths Aptitude Test (for applicants for maths or computer science to Oxford).

November

- Sit BMAT exam in the first week of November if you are applying for medicine (at Oxford or Cambridge) or veterinary science (Cambridge only).
- Deadline for sitting LNAT (for people who want to study law at Oxford) is at the beginning of November.
- Receive letter inviting you to interview from Oxford or Cambridge and explaining if and when to submit written work. Alternatively you may receive a letter rejecting you at this point.
- Submit written work with the special form – see faculty website for details. (Work should be sent directly to the college unless you have made an 'open application', in which case send it directly to the faculty. The work should be marked by your school).

December

- If invited, attend interview in the first three weeks of December (see precise interview dates for your subject in the prospectus).
- You may have to sit some tests at interview.
- At Cambridge you may have to sit the TSA.
- Before 25 December – hear outcome of application from Oxford.

January

- Beginning of January – applicants who have been placed in the 'winter pool' are notified (Cambridge only). This may or may not entail going to Cambridge for another set of interviews.
- Middle of January – hear outcome of application from Cambridge.

June

- Sit A levels.
- After A levels sit STEP paper or AEA (maths only).

August

- Mid-August – results day.
- If you have made your grades your place will be confirmed by the university.
- If you have not made your grades, contact the admissions tutor for your college.
- You may be sent a letter of rejection at this point.

Appendix 2: glossary

Admissions tutor. The tutor especially assigned the role of selecting candidates.

Alumni. People who once went to the college but who have now graduated.

Clearing. When the A level exam results come out in August, students who do not make their offers or, alternatively, students who get much better grades than predicted, can enter a competition for places at universities that have spare places.

Collections. Exams sat at the beginning of each term at Oxford in the colleges.

Collegiate system. This term describes the fact that both Oxford and Cambridge Universities are divided into about 30 separate colleges, where students live and where their social lives are based.

Deferred entry. This means you would like to take a gap year (i.e. defer your entry for a year). You apply this year but will accept a place in two years' time.

Deselected. Some candidates will not have made it to the interview; they are 'deselected' before the interview and will receive a letter of rejection.

DOS. Director of Studies at Cambridge University. Your DOS is an academic member of staff from your subject faculty, who is also a fellow of your college. He or she is responsible for your academic development and will meet with you at the beginning and end of each term to check on your progress and will probably be your interviewer. The DOS at Cambridge is the equivalent to a tutor at Oxford.

Exhibitions. A scholarship you can win in recognition of outstanding work at Oxford.

Faculty. The department building dedicated to one particular subject, for example, the Faculty of Architecture.

Fellow. A 'fellow' is an academic member of a college. Each academic in every faculty is also assigned a college; this is where their office space is located. Some more senior 'fellows' are given responsibility for the academic achievement of the students at their college and act as the DOS (at Cambridge) or tutor (at Oxford) of a number of undergraduates.

Fresher. First year undergraduate student.

Go up. Traditionally, instead of simply saying 'go to university' for Oxford and Cambridge the verb used is to 'go up' to university.

Open application. A way of applying to either Oxford or Cambridge without specifying a college.

Oxbridge. The collective term for Oxford and Cambridge.

Permanent private halls. These are like mini-colleges in Oxford, two of them (St Benet's Hall (men only) and Regent's Park College (men and women)) are for students studying any subject, but the remaining five are mainly for people who are training to be in the ministry.

Pool. The pool is the place where applicants who are rejected by their first-choice college are held until another college selects them for an interview. The other college may do this for a variety of reasons, such as if they have not got enough good applicants and want to find some better ones, or if they want to check that their weakest chosen student is better than another college's rejected student – a sort of moderation process.

Porter's lodge. Your first port of call at an Oxford or Cambridge college. This is where post gets delivered and where, if you get lost, they will be able to direct you – a bit like reception.

Porters. The porters are the men and women who act like wardens of the lodge.

Read. Instead of 'studying' a subject, the verb used is to 'read' a subject.

Subfusc. The black gown, black trousers/skirt and white shirts Oxford students must wear to take exams.

Summon. Another way to say 'to be called' for interview.

Supervision. A class held on a one-to-one basis or in a small group with your tutor (in Cambridge).

Tripos. Word used to describe how Cambridge degree courses are divided into blocks of one or two years, called Part I and Part II.

Tutor. At Oxford University your tutor is an academic member of staff from your subject faculty, who is also a fellow of your college. He or she is responsible for your academic development and will meet with you on a regular basis to check on your progress, and will probably be your interviewer. The DOS at Cambridge is the equivalent to a tutor at Oxford.

Tutorial. A class held on a one-to-one basis or in a small group with your tutor (in Oxford).

Appendix 3: the UCAS form

1| Go to www.ucas.com/students/apply to register in September. In order to do this you will need an email address. If you haven't got one go to yahoo.com or hotmail.com and get a free one. When you register on the UCAS website, you will be sent an application number, user name and password, which you will need every time you log on to UCAS.

2| The entire application is done online and although it may seem complex and time consuming, you can complete it in stages and come back to it. There are 'help' sections all the way through the form in case you get stuck.

3| Fill in the 'Personal details' section, which includes your name, address and date of birth.

4| Fill in the 'Student support' section, which is where you have to select your fee code. If you are a British national your local authority will be your fee payer.

5| Next is an 'Additional information' section in which you can list the activities you have done in preparation for further education. These activities specifically refer to attending summer schools in preparation for university run by either the universities themselves or trusts such as the Sutton Trust. See www.suttontrust.com/index.asp or contact UCAS for more information (www.ucas.com/about_us/contact_us).

6| The fifth section is where you enter your 'University choices'. You can apply to either Oxford or Cambridge. Choose the correct university code from the drop-down menu (CAM C05 for Cambridge and OXF 033 for Oxford). You also need to write what UCAS calls the 'campus code', which is the college code. A drop-down list will appear again. You will also need to choose the subject and select which year of entry you are applying for.

7| The next section asks you for details of your education. You need to write down every GCSE and A level (or equivalent qualification) you have taken and what grade you got under the heading of the school in which you took them. If you are applying post-A level you need to write down all of your module grades.

8| The next section is 'Employment'. This does not ask you about work experience, but about paid employment. It is worth writing down even the most insignificant jobs you have done – washing dishes at the local restaurant, for example – since admissions tutors will value the commitment and maturity you will have shown when holding down a job.

9| Next is the 'Personal Statement'. This is your chance to show the admissions tutors how you write and how informed you are about your subject. You should write this in a Word document, spell check it and read it through carefully and when it is ready, copy and paste it into the UCAS form. The Personal Statement is discussed in more detail in Chapter 3.

10| Finally, send the form off in the first week of October to be completed by your teachers (it goes to your teacher). In order to do this, you have to pay £19 (or £9 if you are applying to just one university) to UCAS to process your information. This must be paid by credit card (your school may have a policy of paying this for you so you need to check before you part with any money). Your teacher will then be able to open it on the teachers' part of the UCAS site. They will read it to check everything is correct and will then write their reference and predicted grades. Your teacher may need some time to write the reference, so do make sure you have your part done well in advance.

11| Your teachers then need to send your UCAS form to Oxford and Cambridge by 15 October. This will arrive at the universities immediately.

Appendix 4: maps

Oxford map

Cambridge map

Fitzwilliam

New Hall

St Edmund's

Girton

Lucy
Cavendish

◀ Churchill

CASTLE STREET

CHESTERTON LANE

N

Magdalene

MAGDALENE ST

Jesus

JESUS LANE

St John's

Trinity

Sidney
Sussex

BRIDGE ST

Bus
Station

Christ's

GARRET HOSTEL LANE

Caius

Robinson

GRANGE ROAD

QUEEN'S ROAD

Trinity
Hall

Clare

King's

Corpus
Christi

Emmanuel

Homerton
Hughes Hall ◀

St Catharine's

Queens'

SILVER STREET

TRUMPINGTON

Pembroke

Downing

Selwyn

Peterhouse

STREET

Newnham

FEN CAUSEWAY

Railway
Station

◀ Wolfson

Postscript

If you have followed the advice in this book then you will have certainly given Oxford or Cambridge your best shot. Good luck and remember that you will be successful at whichever university you attend.

MPW (London)
90–92 Queen's Gate
London
SW7 5AB
Tel: 020 7835 1355
Fax: 020 7259 2705
Email: enquiries@mpw.co.uk